UNLOCKING
THE MYSTERY OF THE
BOOK OF
REVELATION

The unveiling of what was sealed

John Shorey

www.Tribulationtruth.com

Copyright page

Unlocking the Mystery of the book of Revelation

By John Shorey

www.tribulationtruth.com

ISBN: 978-0-578-13525-0

Acknowledgements

**I would like to give a special thanks
to Kevin Shorey and Jim Bakker
for recognizing the importance
of the message of my first book,
<u>The Window of the Lord's Return</u>
And thank them for opening doors so the
message God has given me could go
forth.**

I would also like to thank all those who have helped me
from the beginning. Many giving more hours than
could be imagined and thank you to the many that
have been a great encouragement to me, cheering me
on as I have pushed forward in what I have seen as a
God given assignment.

Table of Contents

About the Author

Shawnette and I met while attending Northwest Bible College in Kirkland, Washington in 1977. We were married in 1978 and reared two boys who are serving God. Shawnette and I gave most of our service to God by ministering to children. We spent five years traveling across the country as evangelists to children and their families. We also spent many years as children's pastors and currently reside in Arizona. I sensed God's directing me to write my first book, the strongest tug by God's Holy Spirit that I have ever experienced. In an attitude of obedience, I have been diligent to complete this assignment. I had no thought of writing a second book, but God led me to this new study and when I shared it with others I realized that by publishing this book, it would reach the largest audience that this study deserves.

Always in His Service,
John Shorey

Preface

At twenty years of age in 1972 I was preparing to leave on what I considered a great adventure. I had worked on a farm for seven seasons while finishing my school years and now I was headed to Fairbanks Alaska to go to college.

This adventure was any young man's dream come true. I ended up in Ketchikan as a logger for several years and in 1974 I came to know the Lord Jesus as my Savior. I was continuing my college years at the University of Alaska during the winter months when the logging operations would be shut down. Then in 1976 I started attending Northwest Bible College in Kirkland, Washington. While attending Northwest College I met the girl of my dreams.

At about this time I was sharing with my mother how I was happy with the choices I had made in life, she told me something that I never forgot. She said that I had always marched to the beat of my own drum; I was never one who followed the crowd. Recently I was reflecting on this and I realized that it is now my desire to march to the beat of the heart of God, and to seek with my whole heart to hear his heart beat that I may follow Him in obedience.

Too many Christians today are listening to the wrong drums and the beat is too loud to hear the still small voice of God. Do we want to be known as one who follows the crowd, a man pleaser or a God pleaser?

Even among Christian leaders today, I see too many who do not want to rock the boat. Jesus would rock the boat if need be, remember he knocked over all the tables and chased the money changers out of the temple.

In these last days, it is time to be bold. Shadrach, Meshach and Abed-nego stood tall for what they believed and refused to follow the crowd, even if it meant taking some heat. If we are not willing to take a stand at times, when we know we are right, how can we expect God to step into the furnace and vindicate us?

Letters from readers of this study

Hi John,

I finished reading Revelation in the chronological order into which you placed everything. I read very slowly, digesting small amounts at a time. For the first time, the book of Revelation makes sense to me. Previously, reading it in the order presented in the Bible, it was confusing to me because it felt disjointed with things out of place. Thank you for the time, effort, and obedience to bring the Lord's message to His people.

Evangelist Ken

HI John,

Bravo for you. I just finished reading Revelation where you plug in the 6 chapters in chronological order and it fits beautifully. I had a brief discussion with you after I read your book about Rev.14 being a perfect picture of the rapture of the Church as something I have seen for many years. However, I did not have it in its proper place and I had taken a rapture position of, "at the last Trump" from Rev.10, but I was not fully persuaded because of the things happening in Rev. 8. Now YOU have made perfect sense to it all or rather the Lord has now revealed it to you in its proper place. Thank you and God bless you.

Tom

Hello John,
The insights you have shared placing the book of Revelation in chronological order, I believe is supernatural and could only have come to you via the Holy Spirit. I feel gratitude that I was allowed to learn this.

Scott

God Bless you as you study and search for truth.

A Servant in Christ Jesus,
John Shorey.
www.tribulationtruth.com

Unlocking the Mystery of the Book of Revelation

By John Shorey, with much help from the Holy Spirit.

The book of Revelation is the only book in the Bible that has a promised blessing to those who read it. I believe, to qualify for this blessing, you need to give the book of Revelation a serious read, praying for God to help you understand the important message of this book. The book of Revelation is not your typical book of the Bible, for Jesus appeared in a vision to John and gave him the contents of this book. If you will follow along with me on this study, **I will show you that it was not just Jesus who gave John the book of Revelation, but John was interrupted twice by an angel who gave John further revelation.** What I will show you concerning these two interruptions by an angel is that what they gave John was revelation that was out of the chronological order of what Jesus was revealing to John. I will conclude by showing how we can reposition these angelic revelations in chronological order as sort of footnotes that will further illuminate the revelation that Jesus was revealing to John.

Some say the book of Revelation is too confusing to be understood, thus causing many to avoid reading it all together. I have even heard Bible teachers say the book of Revelation is allegorical and not relevant for us today. I would take issue with anyone who would dare say that any of God's Word would be irrelevant. I liken the book of Revelation to the parables Jesus used to teach his disciples and followers. Jesus disciples asked him one time why Jesus taught in parables. Jesus answered them in Mark 4:10-12, (NIV), *"When he was alone, the Twelve and the others around him asked him about the parables. He told them, "The secret of the kingdom of God has been given to you. But to those on the outside everything is said in parables so that, they may be ever seeing but never perceiving, and ever hearing but never understanding..."*

Both Daniel, who wrote the book of Daniel, and John, who wrote the book of Revelation, was told that mysteries and questions from these books would be sealed until the time of the end. I believe with all my heart that we are now at the time of the end. In fact, I believe we have already entered the birth pains of the last days. I believe we are now at the time that God is unveiling the secrets that have been sealed in God's Holy Word.

Before I go into my teaching I want to show from the first chapter of Revelation that it was Jesus who appeared to John while John was in the spirit on the Lord's Day.

Revelation 1:10-13, (NIV), *"On the Lord's Day I was in the Spirit, and I heard behind me a loud voice like a trumpet, which said, "Write on a scroll what you see and send it to the seven churches: to Ephesus, Smyrna, Pergamum, Thyatira, Sardis, Philadelphia and Laodicea." I turned around to see the voice that was speaking to me. And when I turned I saw seven golden lampstands, and among the lampstands was someone "like a son of man," dressed in a robe reaching down to his feet and with a golden sash around his chest."*

Now, I will show that the first chapter of Revelation also teaches that this message would be verified and further testified to by angels. Read Revelation 1:1-2 (NIV), *"The Revelation of Jesus Christ, which God gave him to show his servants what must soon take place. He made it known by sending his angel to his servant John, who testifies to everything he saw—that is, the word of God and the testimony of Jesus Christ."*

As I have studied the book of Revelation, I have seen that there are places in this book that are not in chronological order. When I discovered this, I realized that because part of the book of Revelation is out of sequence, this has led to many misinterpretations of the Book of Revelation. For instance, there are at least five different interpretations for the timing of the rapture. We need to realize that only one of these teachings can be correct.

The first realization I had that not all of the book of Revelation was in chronological order happened when I was writing the book, The Window of the Lord's Return. I was reading Revelation 14:1 (NIV). *"Then I looked and there before me was the Lamb, standing on Mount Zion, and with him 144,000 who had his name and his Father's name written on their foreheads."* This verse really confused me. This verse is showing Jesus visiting with the 144,000 specially chosen Jews on mount Zion, before Jesus returns and places his feet on the Mount of Olives. The Bible clearly teaches that Jesus' first contact back on Earth will be when his feet touch down on the Mount of Olives. When I read this, I prayed and asked God to show me why this did not make sense. I determined to read through the book of Revelation until God would reveal why this confusion was here. On my third read, the Holy Spirit opened my eyes to what was going on.

If you will read Revelation chapter 10, you will see that an angel interrupts John and gives him a second smaller scroll. (Realize that when John was called to write the book of Revelation, he saw Jesus in a vision while he was in the spirit, and Jesus gave John the revelation of the last days.) When John was interrupted by the angel, the angel told John to write again about things John had already written about. Revelation 10:11 (NIV), *"Then I was told, "You must prophecy again about many peoples, nations, languages and kings."* When I read this sequence where the angel interrupted John, I realized that John had been writing about the wrath of God in the form of the seven trumpets of God's wrath. I realized that when God starts pouring out his wrath on unrepentant man, God is not going to take a break in his outpouring of wrath. This was one of the clues that made me realize that Revelations chapters 11- 14 were out of chronological order.

When I realized what had happened here, I realized that this portion of Revelation that was given to John by the angel was covering a timeline that was all over the place. Jesus meeting with the 144,000 Jews does not take place until after Jesus touches the earth at the Mount of Olives. (This event probably happens after the victory of the Battle of Armageddon.) The portion that is talking about war in heaven and Satan being thrown to the earth should appear just before the antichrist is revealed. The portion where it says one of the heads of the beast is fatally wounded happens at the opening of the first seal, because this is the event that leads to Satan's becoming the antichrist. Many other portions from chapters 11-14 are also out of chronological order.

When God revealed all this to me some time ago, I did not realize the full significance of what was happening here. It was not until a few weeks ago when I was doing further study in the book of Revelation that God illuminated His

Word for me to see that there was a second instance where John was interrupted by an angel. We find this at the end of Revelation 16, where John is finishing his description of the seven bowl judgments. After the seven bowl judgments have been completed. **What should follow after the completion of the wrath of God?** This should be where Jesus mounts his white horse, and the saints will follow him back to the earth for the battle of Armageddon. But this is not what follows in the book of Revelation. **Revelation 17:1 shows an angel interrupting John,** and the angel shows him the punishment of the great prostitute. Read Revelation17:1 (NIV). *"One of the seven angels who had the seven bowls came and said to me, "Come, I will show you the punishment of the great prostitute, who sits on many waters."* Chapters 17 and 18 continue with the angel telling John about Mystery Babylon. In Chapter 18:4 (NIV), the angel is saying, *"Come out of her my people, so that you will not share in her sins, so that you will not receive any of her plagues."* As the angel continues to share with John into the end of chapter 18, the angel is talking about the destruction of Mystery Babylon. Then chapter 18 finishes with information about the martyrdom of the saints.

When I read this, I realized that this was a second account given to John by the angel that is not in chronological order. Why would God have to say, "Come out of her my people" in Revelation chapter 18, if God had already completed His wrath at the end of Revelation chapter 16? If you will continue reading to Revelation 19:11, this is where you will see the chronological account of the book of Revelation continue. For this is where you see Jesus riding the white horse with the saints following Him to the final battle of Armageddon. Read Revelation19:11 (NIV), *"I saw heaven standing open and there before me was a white horse, whose rider is called Faithful and True. With justice he judges and makes war."* Then verse 14, (NIV) *"The armies of heaven were following him, riding on white horses and dressed in fine linen, white and clean."*

This is when it dawned on me that the account that Jesus gave to John is all in chronological order, but the two instances where John is interrupted by the angel, these portions of the book of Revelation are not in chronological order. This was truly another WOW moment for me. It was at this point that I realized that if I read the book of Revelation through and skipped over the two instances where John was interrupted by an angel, I would get a chronological snapshot of the book of Revelation. The Revelation given to John by Jesus is the foundation of the book of Revelation. What the angels revealed to John is what I see as additional footnotes or overlays to give a clearer understanding of the end times.

When this dawned on me that what the angel shared with John was not placed in the book of Revelation in chronological order, the next thought I had was, "What would happen if we could place these angelic interruptions in chronological order?" So I found a Word document of the book of Revelation and started taking the steps to place this extra information provided by the angel into chronological order.

The first step I took was to remove the first interruption that happened at the end of the 6th trumpet of God's wrath. This interruption included chapters 11-14.

(The instructions in Chapter 10 concerning this information, where it describes the little scroll, I decided to leave in its original place.) When this interruption is moved out of the way, what you see is the account of God's wrath that was being played out in chapters 8 and 9 continuing into Revelation chapters 15 and 16. I moved this portion of Revelation that was the angelic interruption to the end of the book of Revelation, so I could move it back later. (**Realize that if Revelation 11-14 is not in chronological order, then there must be a placement that is in chronological order**). I then took chapters 17, 18, and 19:1-10 and moved this portion to the end of Revelation. Next I closed up the spaces that were made by taking out these portions that were from the angelic interruptions. When this was done, what I had was the revelation that Jesus gave to John. This was what I now call the foundation for the book of Revelation, and the information that the angel gave to John will become foot notes or overlays that will complement the information that Jesus gave to John.

Now I realize that some will say that you cannot take apart or rearrange the Word of God. I will remind you that when you do a study in God's Word, it is common to use Scripture from many books in the Bible. The four Gospels share the same basic story but from the different perspectives of Jesus' disciples. Scholars have written a study on the Gospels where they take all the different accounts and assemble each different account to make a complete story of the Gospels. This is called harmonizing the Gospels. I am basically harmonizing the book of Revelation by putting it into chronological order. **Please realize I am not adding one word or taking away one word from the book of Revelation**; I am arranging the book in chronological order.

The next step was to look at these two interruptions and determine where these portions of Scripture belong, so that the book of Revelation may be read and understood in chronological order. When you look at the two angelic interruptions, the first interruption found in Revelation chapters 11-14, have many segments that contain different topics that will need to be matched with many different locations in order to arrange the book of Revelation in chronological order. The second angelic interruption found in Chapters 17 – 19:10 is already in chronological order, but this portion of Revelation was still not placed in its chronological location.

I have already explained why Revelation Chapters 17-19:10 is not placed in its chronological location, but what I need to point out is how I know this portion belongs together in one section. If you read Revelation 17, you will see that the topic is about the prostitute and Mystery Babylon. When you get to the end of chapter 17, you will notice it says, "After this", these words connect chapter 17 to chapter 18. Then when you read chapter 18, at the end of this chapter, you will notice it uses these same words again, "After this…". This is connecting the end of chapter 18 with chapter 19. Then when you start reading chapter 19, and you read down to Revelation 19:11, this is where you see the rider on the white horse appear. This is where Jesus is coming to the earth for the Battle of Armageddon with the saints following, riding on white horses. As I said earlier, this is the event that would logically follow the end of the wrath of God that was completed in Revelation chapter 16. This is why it makes sense that this angelic interruption ends just before this event found in Revelation 19:11.

Now that we have identified that this second interruption runs from Revelation 17 through 19:10, we now need to find the place where this portion of Revelation belongs. When you realize that a portion of the book of Revelation is misplaced, you now need to determine where it should be placed.

What I have determined is that you must look for a place in the Revelation account that Jesus gave to John that matches the subject, topic or key words. To make a match, I determined that a match must be found to correspond with either the first sentence or paragraph of the portion of Scripture that is out of order, or you will look for a match at the end of the portion that is out of order. In the case of Revelation 17-19:10, the beginning is talking about the prostitute, and there is no match. So then you must look at what is the topic at the end of this portion and you look for a place in the revelation of Jesus that matches. The end of this portion found in Revelation 19:1-10 is about an event that is happening in heaven.

When I study Revelation chapter 7, I see several matches. Revelation 19:1 (NIV) talks about a **roar** or loud noise, and a **great multitude**. When you read Revelation 7:9 (NIV) you see the key words "**great multitude**" and the phrase, "**cried out in a loud voice**". As you continue reading Rev.19:1-2 (NIV) you see the phrase, "**Salvation and glory and power belong to our God**". Then in Revelation chapter 7:10 (NIV) "**Salvation belongs to our God**". Both Revelation chapter 19:1-10 and Revelation chapter 7 are talking about an event taking place in heaven with elders around the throne.

Both of these portions of Revelation in chapter 7 and 19 are talking about the same topic. But what I see as my final convincing clues that Revelation 17-19:10 belongs as a further footnote to give us a clearer understanding of the book of Revelation is found with the following match. Revelation 19:7-8 (NIV), *"Let us rejoice and be glad and give him glory! For the wedding of the Lamb has come, and **his bride has made herself ready. Fine linen, bright and clean, was given her to wear.**"* Then read,

Revelation 7:13-14 (NIV), *"Then one of the elders asked me, "These in white robes-who are they, and where did they come from?" I answered, "Sir you know." And he said, "These are they who have come out of the great tribulation:* **they have washed their robes and made them white in the blood of the Lamb.** *"*

In conclusion, when I realized that Revelation 17-19:10 fits into the Revelation account found in Revelation chapter 7, this is where I have seen the rapture occurring. Both of these accounts are talking about the saints in heaven in white linen and you realize that the marriage supper of the Lamb is about to take place.

Another realization that hit me was when I realized that Revelation 17 and 18, concerning the destruction of Mystery Babylon, comes before the rapture event (described in Revelation 19:1-10). This is made clear because Rev.19:1-10 is now located in chapter 7 at what is now looking more like a rapture event then what we have seen before reading the book of Revelation in chronological order. This was an eye-opener for me. I have always believed that Mystery Babylon is the United States. And when you see the destruction of Mystery Babylon happening before the rapture, need I say more?

There will be hard times before we are taken out of here in the rapture. I cover why I see the United States could be Mystery Babylon in my book, The Window of the Lords Return in chapter 4, "How does the United States fit into the prophetic picture?" I will share some portions from this chapter below. I see this is relevant because of what I am uncovering in this study, that Mystery Babylon is destroyed before the rapture.

"Over the years, my thoughts on this subject have led me to see that we have been the main protector of Israel, thus causing the United States to be standing in the way of many of the prophetic events that have to fall into place. As long as the United States is a strong superpower, we would not stand by and let Israel be attacked and destroyed, for we have always provided them with armaments and supplies. This simple line of reasoning has brought me to some interesting options.

1) If we are in the way of prophecy being fulfilled, we could be defeated in a world war, and we would not be around to do any more protecting.

2) The United States would have an economic collapse which would make us so poor that we could no longer hold the position as Israel's protector and as the world cop. Also, our problems would be so severe at home that we would need all our military and police forces to keep things under control at home, thus making it so we would not have the resources to deal with world problems anymore. This is difficult to envision and I do not want to see these kinds of hard times. I certainly do not want to experience an event like the Great Depression of the thirties that hit my father's generation, but I have always believed that for the end-time events to unfold, according to that which has been laid out in the Bible, then America and the world would have to experience a widespread economic collapse.

3) My next option is a long one and the most thought provoking. I have questioned the Scriptures I am about to share with you, wondering for years if these Scriptures could be talking about the United States. If it were not for the fact that I have read other prophetic writers sharing my questions and possible conclusions, I would hesitate to share these thoughts.

Where do we begin? If you read Revelation 18, about the destruction of Mystery Babylon, you have to wonder if America could be a spiritual or a type of the actual, real physical, geographically located Babylon. Most Bible teachers believe these Scriptures are talking about Iraq. But when you carefully read the passage, you will see many Scriptures that show the country of Iraq does not fit the description of the country to be destroyed in judgment.

Here is an example: Revelation 18:10 (NIV) says, *".....Woe! Woe! O great city, O Babylon, city of power! In one hour your doom has come!"* Iraq is not a city of power today; they had their day, and so the question I have is whether these Scriptures are talking about a country that has the spirit of Babylon and not the geographic Iraq of today. Read these Scriptures with that thought in mind and apply the thought that the city of power it is talking about is the United States, then see if it makes sense to you.

For example read, Revelation 17:1-2 (NIV): *"...Come, I will show you the punishment of the great prostitute, who sits on many waters. With her the kings of the earth committed adultery and the inhabitants of the earth were intoxicated with the wine of her adulteries."* Geographically, the USA sits on many waters and contains many peoples from many nationalities, and Iraq does not. Now read, Revelation 17:15 (NIV): *".....The waters you saw, where the prostitute sits, are peoples, multitudes, nations and languages."* America is a land known as a land of many peoples and languages, and Iraq is not. Revelation 17:18 (NIV) says, *"The woman you saw is the great city that rules over the kings of the earth."* This sounds like the USA, not Iraq."

Again, in closing I believe if mystery Babylon is in fact

the United States. We in America need to realize that if this event does in fact happen before the rapture, then we need to prepare for the safety of our families. Some say Mystery Babylon is New York City, the center of wealth in America and the world. This could be true, but even if just New York City is destroyed, it would still bring down the rest of America as we know it today.

Now, we need to look at Revelation chapters 11-14, the first angelic interruption, and see where these four chapters of the revelation fit into the chronological Revelation of Jesus.

As I have studied and pondered how to divide the Book Revelation chapters 11-14, I knew this would not be as easy of an assignment, because these chapters cover many subjects and topics. The time line for these chapters is all over the place as I explained earlier. What I did was study and break these four chapters into separate sections based on the subject matter. When I did this, I came up with nine different sections that I would need to determine where they should fit into the chronological reading of the Book of Revelation. This will also include Revelation 17-19:10 as the tenth section. Each section is in bold type when I move them into chronological order.

Below I have listed the 9 sections from these four chapters.

1. Revelation 11:1 - 11:14 covers the temple and the arrival of the two witnesses.

2. Revelation 11:15 covers the sounding of the Seventh Trumpet.

3. Revelation 11:16 - 11:19 covers the twenty four elders at the throne in heaven.

4. Revelation 12:1 - 13:18 covers Satan's attack against the children of Israel and Satan being cast to the earth.

5. Revelation 14:1 - 14:5 covers the 144,000 meeting with Jesus on Mount Zion.

6. Revelation 14:6 - 14:7 covers an angel warning the people not to take the mark of the beast

7. Revelation 14:8 - 14:13 contains the 2nd and 3rd angels proclaiming the destruction of Babylon and the sentence of judgment for those who take the mark of the beast.

8. Revelation 14:14 - 14:16 contains the first harvest of the earth or the Rapture.

9. Revelation 14:17 - 14:20 contains the harvest of the unrepentant that follows the rapture.

What I decided to do was pick out some of the most significant sections from Revelation chapters 11-14 and show why I believe they fit where I am placing them. I then provide a copy of the King James Version of the book of Revelation that I will use to place these Scripture portions into chronological order. All ten sections from Revelation chapters 11-14 and chapters 17-19:10, are then arranged in chronological order. I have highlighted each portion of Scripture in bold print so you can identify what I have done. I believe that as you read and see how these portions that came from the interruption of angels is arranged in order, you will see a whole new clarity come from your reading and studying this most important message that God has given His church for these Last Days. When you read how I have arranged the Book of Revelation in chronological order, following this you will see a study guide that will show you how to read any translation of the book of Revelation in chronological order.

The first portion that I see as quite significant coming from Revelation chapters 11-14 is found in Rev. 11:1-14. This portion covers the arrival of the two witnesses. This portion of Scripture will be placed in the location that I see as makes the most sense for the time of the arrival of the two witnesses. This portion of Scripture actually covers the whole 3.5 years that they will be on the earth. When you read this portion, you need to take this fact into account that some of the things being said about the two witnesses is speaking ahead 3.5 years to the time of their death. To determine the chronological timing for the two witnesses to arrive, we need to find some clue in this portion of Scripture that links to the time line of Revelation.

If you read to the end of this portion of Scripture, to the time of the death of the two witnesses, you will see that after they come back to life there is a severe earthquake. There are only two severe earthquakes mentioned in the Book of Revelation, one is at the sixth seal and the other is at the seventh bowl of God's wrath. I believe we can eliminate the timing of the sixth seal for the time of the death of the two witnesses because 3.5 years before their death would place their arrival before the arrival of the antichrist. This does not make sense because the judgments they will call down on the earth is more in keeping with the timing of the wrath of God. If you will read in chapter 16, where it describes the seven bowls of God's wrath, you will see the seventh bowl of God's wrath describes an earthquake which will topple the cities of the world. I believe that this event lines up with the timing of the two witnesses coming back to life after being dead for three days. If I am correct, then to find the chronological placement for the arrival of the two witnesses, we have to find a place in the timeline that is 3.5 years before the seventh bowl of God's wrath.

As I have studied the End Times, I have found that not all End Time teachers share the view that the Great Tribulation is 7 years long. I will give a brief description of where I see God's Word teaching that the Great Tribulation is seven years long and then show my reasoning for placing the arrival of the two witnesses where I believe it makes the most sense.

I am of the camp of End Time teachers that believe the Great Tribulation happens during the time of Daniel's seventieth week, also called the last week of years. The teaching of Daniel's seventy weeks comes from the 9th chapter of the book of Daniel. Daniel 9:24 (NIV) introduces the teaching of the seventy weeks. *"Seventy 'sevens' are decreed for your people and your holy city to finish transgression, to put an end to sin,…."*. If you will read Daniel 9:25-26, you will see it discusses the time called 62 weeks and 7 weeks. It says this time frame of 69 weeks will end with
the destruction of the Temple. This event happened in 70 AD, many years after the crucifixion of Jesus.

(An important note to make is, this last week of years cannot have happened during the life of Christ if the first 69 weeks ended after his Crucifixion.)

After the destruction of the temple, we have one last week of years yet to be fulfilled, and if you continue reading in Daniel, you will see this last week of years described. Daniel 9:27 talks of the antichrist confirming a covenant for **one seven**. Dan.9:27 (NIV) *"He will confirm a covenant with many for one 'seven', in the middle of the 'seven' he will put an end to sacrifice and offering..."*. **This one seven being described here is a week of years or seven years.** I have heard some teach that this person referred to as "He will confirm a covenant" is talking about Christ confirming the New Testament covenant at his death 3.5 years from the beginning of his ministry. This cannot be the case when you realize the first sixty-nine weeks ended after the Crucifixion and after the destruction of the temple. The first sixty-nine weeks and the seventieth week will not overlap each other.

Just as a further note on the definition of the Great Tribulation I have been told that the Great Tribulation is only 42 months long and it comprises the war on the saints by the antichrist. I see the first period of 42 months ending at the Rapture as the first half of what I call the Great Tribulation or Daniels seventieth week because after the Rapture when God is pouring out his wrath on the earth, this will still be great tribulation for the unrepentant.

Now if some would prefer to call the first 3.5 years the Great Tribulation and the second 3.5 years the wrath of God, as long as you see the total as seven years, equaling Daniels seventieth week of years, then we are in agreement. In <u>The Window of the Lord's Return</u>, I have done a study from Daniel 12, that shows two distinct 3.5 year periods, that adds up to the 7 year tribulation period. I will place a portion of this study below.

"Notice this verse (Revelation 13:5) says he, the antichrist was given authority for forty-two months. Some have taken this to mean that the antichrist would only appear on the scene for forty-two months. This does not make sense because the antichrist makes a seven year peace with Israel and breaks it in the middle. Now what this verse is saying is the same as what Daniel chapter seven is saying. The antichrist has been given authority over the saints for forty-two months and after that period, just as Daniel 7:21-22 (NIV) says God intervenes. *"As I watched, this horn was waging war against the saints and defeating them, until the Ancient of Days came and pronounced judgment in favor of the saints of the Most High, and the time came when they possessed the kingdom."*

If you read Daniel 12:1-2, you will realize these verses are talking about the time of the Great Tribulation. These verses then describe a deliverance from this time of Great Tribulation. (Notice that Michael the archangel is standing up and ready to play a part in this coming deliverance.) What is the form of this deliverance that is being referred to? If you will notice who are included in this event, you will realize it must be talking about the rapture of the saints. Read Daniel 12:1-2, (NIV): *"At that time Michael the great prince who protects your people, will arise. There will be a time of distress such as has not happened from the beginning of nations until then. But at that time your people – everyone whose name is found written in the book – will be delivered. Multitudes who sleep in the dust of the earth will awake: some to everlasting life, others to shame and everlasting contempt."*

When you see the dead in Christ who have their names written in the Book of Life, awakening from the sleep of death, clearly the event described here is the Rapture. Read 1 Thessalonians 4:15-18 (NIV): *"According to the*

Lord's own word, we tell you that we who are still alive, who are left till the coming of the Lord, will certainly not precede those who have fallen asleep. For the Lord himself will come down from heaven, with a loud command, with the voice of the archangel and with the trumpet call of God, and the dead in Christ will rise first. After that, we who are still alive and are left will be caught up together with them in the clouds to meet the Lord in the air. And so we will be with the Lord forever. Therefore encourage each other with these words."

This is a WOW moment for me. When you read above where it says, *"For the Lord himself will come down from heaven, with a loud command, with the voice of the archangel..."* Michael is the archangel, one of the top generals in command of the armies of God, and Daniel 12:1 shows Michael getting ready to play his part in the rapture of all those whose names are written in the Book of Life, who are the elect of God, or the saints.

It is interesting that after these coming events were described in Daniel 12:1-2, it goes on to say in Daniel 12:4, that these words were to be sealed up until the time of the end. Daniel 12:4 (NIV): *"But you, Daniel, close up and seal the words of the scroll until the time of the end..."* If you read further, it gets very interesting, as verses 5-7 describe two men standing on both sides of the river talking to a man in linen that was above them. I believe the man in linen was Jesus and the other two may have been Michael, the archangel, and maybe another angel.

One of the men or an angel asks the question, *"How long will it be before these astonishing things are fulfilled?"* What are the astonishing things referred to? The things referred to in Daniel 12:1-2 are the time of the Great

Tribulation up until the time of the deliverance of God's people whose names are written in the Book of Life, both the living and those who are dead in the Lord. Then the man in linen – who I believe is Jesus – answers the question and describes this time as *"a time, times, and half a time"*, (or three and one- half years). This places the Rapture three and one-half years into the Great Tribulation.

Now read Daniel 12:5-8 and see if what I am saying makes sense. Daniel 12:5-8 (NIV): *"Then I Daniel, looked, and there before me stood two others, one on this bank of the river and one on the opposite bank. One of them said to the man clothed in linen, who was above the waters of the river, 'How long will it be before these astonishing things are fulfilled?' The man clothed in linen who was above the waters of the river, lifted his right hand and his left hand toward heaven, and I heard him swear by him who lives forever, saying, "It will be for a time, times, and half a time. When the power of the holy people has been finally broken, all these things will be completed."*

Again notice the last part of the answer from the man in linen. It says that once the power of the holy people has been broken, all these things will be completed. Realize that during this time of the Great Tribulation, the antichrist has been waging war against the saints. About this time, the antichrist will enter the temple and declare that he is God.

Now get the picture of what is happening here. Daniel just had it explained to him how long it would be until these astonishing things would be fulfilled. However, Daniel still does not get the full picture. So again he asks another question. The question is not about the fulfillment of the astonishing things but about the outcome of all of these things. Read Daniel 12:8-11 (NIV): *"I heard, but I did not understand. So I asked, "My Lord, what will the outcome of all this be?"* He replied, *"Go your way, Daniel, because the words are closed up and sealed until the time of the end. Many will be purified, made spotless and refined, but the wicked will continue to be wicked. None of the wicked will understand, but those who are wise will understand. From the time that the daily sacrifice is abolished and the abomination that causes desolation is set up, there will be 1,290 days."*

This is another revelation moment for me. Daniel has had two questions answered in Daniel chapter 12. The first question concerned the time when the astonishing things would be fulfilled. He was told it would be three and one-half years to the time that the saints would be delivered coinciding with the antichrist desecrating the temple. Then Daniel asks what the outcome of all this would be. The Kings James Version v.8 says, "....What shall be the end of these things?" He was told it will be three and one-half years from the time that the daily sacrifice is abolished, the same time that the antichrist is desecrating the temple, until all these things will come to their end. The answers to these two questions have established two things: how long from the beginning of the Great Tribulation to the deliverance of the saints (three and one-half years) and how long from the desecrating of the temple until the end of these things, again (three and a half years). I believe God's Word in Daniel 12 supports my conclusion that the rapture of the church occurs in the middle of the seven- year Great Tribulation period.

Based on what I have shown here, that the tribulation period is seven years long and the two witnesses are killed and rise from the dead just before the end of the seven years, this would mean that they have to show up just before the middle of the seven year period. From this deduction, the arrival of the two witnesses is approximately the time of the sealing of the 144,000 specially chosen and sealed Jews from the twelve tribes of Israel. I go into greater detail on the timing of the Rapture and the arrival of the 144,000 Jews in my book, The Window of the Lord's Return.

The second set of verses coming from the first angelic interruption that I see as quite significant comes from Revelation 11:16-19. This portion of Scripture comes on the heels of the arrival of the two witnesses. When you read Revelation 11:16-19 you will see the topic and key words give strong evidence that this could be talking about the Rapture. Read Revelation 11:18, "*The nations were angry; and your wrath has come. The time has come for judging the dead, and for rewarding your servants the prophets and your saints and those who reverence your name, both small and great - and for destroying those who destroy the earth.*"

As I studied these verses, where it says, "*...The time for judging the dead and rewarding your servants the prophets and your saints and those who reverence your name...*", is an event that will happen at the time of the Rapture. As you continue to study these verses, the end of this portion of Scripture is speaking of the judgment and wrath of God that will follow the time of God rewarding His prophets and saints. I see this as a time of judgment and a time of rewarding in the same breath because both of these aspects are mentioned in this same verse. Read the end of Revelation 11:18. "*...and for destroying those who destroy the earth.*" If you will look at the first words of verse 18, it says, "*The Nations were angry and your wrath has come...*". When I look at this section of Scripture as a whole, I see it is talking about a time of rewarding the saints and at the same time, the time has come for pouring out the wrath of God.

In my study, The Window of the Lords Return, I show the rapture happening at the seventh seal. As you study the opening of the 7th seal you see this is the time when the seven trumpets are handed to the seven angels who are at the throne of God. For this reason I believe the best choice to place this portion of Revelation is following what I see as the arrival of the Saints at the throne as described in Revelation 7:9 – 8:1.

Another reason for placing this portion of Scripture at the opening of the 7th seal is, if you read the first verse in this portion of Scripture, it is talking about the twenty-four elders. When you read the last half of chapter seven of Revelation that leads up to the opening of the 7th seal, it is one of the twenty-four elders that is doing most of the communicating.

I believe the most convincing reason for placing this portion of the angelic interruption at the opening of the 7th seal is based on the last verse in this portion of Scripture, Revelation 11:19b, *"And there came **flashes of lightning, rumblings, peals of thunder,** an **earthquake** and a great **hailstorm**."*

When I was looking for the proper home for this portion of Scripture, I remembered seeing common key words at the end of the opening of the seventh seal. When I read Revelation 8:5 it almost took my breath away. Every key word but one was mentioned. Read Revelation 8:5 (NIV) *"Then the angel took the censer, filled it with fire from the alter, and hurled it on the earth; and there came **peals of thunder, rumblings,*** *flashes of lightning and an earthquake.*"

The only key word missing from the opening of the seventh seal was the hailstorm. Then the thought hit me, "Could the first trumpet contain a severe hail storm? When I read the opening of the first trumpet, there it was. Revelation 8:7 (NIV) *"The first angel sounded his trumpet, and there came **hail** and fire mixed with blood...".*

In closing, the topic and key words of this portion of the angelic interruption are close to a perfect match to where I have positioned them. When you read my chronological rendition of the book of Revelation, I believe you will agree that placing this portion of Scripture here throws much light on what is happening at this time.

A third portion of Scripture from the angelic interruptions that I see as significant comes from Revelation 14:1-5. This is the event where Jesus, the Lamb, is standing on Mount Zion with the 144,000 specially chosen Jews. I mentioned this earlier, as this was the first event that caught my attention that could not have been in chronological order. As I mentioned earlier, the Bible clearly teaches that Jesus' first contact to planet earth will be when Jesus returns to the Mount of Olives, the location that his disciples witnessed His leaving. Other prophecies have said that when He returns and His feet touch the Mount of Olives, the mountain will split from East to West. It was this fact from the Bible that prompted me to study further, which led to what I believe was the Holy Spirit's turning the light bulb on that allowed me to understand what was happening.

When you think about this meeting with Jesus and the 144,000 on Mount Zion, it gets interesting because as they were meeting with Jesus, the Bible says in Rev. 14:2-3 (NIV) that they heard the sounds of music coming from the throne in heaven. *"And I heard a sound from heaven like the roar of rushing waters and like a loud peal of thunder. The sound I heard like that of a harpists playing their harps. And they sang a new song before the throne and before the four living creatures and the elders..."*.

I believe this meeting between Jesus and the 144,000 is a special meeting Jesus arranged to give a special thank you to those who were chosen for a special mission. Jesus is honoring them for a job well done. The Battle of Armageddon would now be over, and it is transition time for us to move from the battle ground of earth to the throne in heaven. If you read this carefully, you can see it shows Jesus meeting the 144,000 at Mount Zion and then leading them to the throne to worship God. I chose Revelation chapter 20 for the placement for this portion of Scripture, because this is where the transition occurs after the Battle of Armageddon is over. I actually placed this portion of Scripture between Revelation 20:3 and 4. When you read this paragraph you see the devil is seized and bound and thrown into the Abyss. Then in verse four, we are seeing the throne in heaven. This location is the transition spot where we see the scene change from the end of the war against evil and Satan, to the place of our eternal reward in heaven. Again this is close to a perfect match, and illuminates the Revelation story.

There are several more portions of Scripture that were separated by topic and subject from the first angelic interruption found in Revelation chapters 11-14. I have shown how I determined the chronological placement of what I considered the most important portions from these chapters. When you read my chronological rendition of the

Book of Revelation, all these portions are highlighted for you to see where they were moved to. I believe as you read this chronological reading of the Book of Revelation, you will agree that arranging these portions of Scriptures that came from the angelic interruptions as foot notes, bring great clarity to the revelation that Jesus gave to John.

At the beginning of this study, I mentioned that much confusion has come from different interpretations of the book of Revelation. This has led to many different teachings on the Lord's return. I believe seeing and reading the book of Revelation in chronological order will do much to illuminate the truth of the Lord's return. My in-depth study on the subject of the Lord's return can be found in my book, The Window of the Lord's Return.

In the following pages you can read the book of Revelation in chronological order after I have applied what I have discussed above.

The Book of Revelation in Chronological Order

Prologue

Rev. 1:1 – 5:14

1 The Revelation of Jesus Christ, which God gave unto him, to shew unto his servants things which must shortly come to pass; and he sent and signified [it] by his angel unto his servant John:

2 Who bare record of the word of God, and of the testimony of Jesus Christ, and of all things that he saw.

3 Blessed [is] he that readeth, and they that hear the words of this prophecy, and keep those things which are written therein: for the time [is] at hand.

4 John to the seven churches which are in Asia: Grace [be] unto you, and peace, from him which is, and which was, and which is to come; and from the seven Spirits which are before his throne;

5 And from Jesus Christ, [who is] the faithful witness, [and] the first begotten of the dead, and the prince of the kings of the earth. Unto him that loved us, and

washed us from our sins in his own blood,

6 And hath made us kings and priests unto God and his Father; to him [be] glory and dominion for ever and ever. Amen.

7 Behold, he cometh with clouds; and every eye shall see him, and they [also] which pierced him: and all kindreds of the earth shall wail because of him. Even so, Amen.

8 I am Alpha and Omega, the beginning and the ending, saith the Lord, which is, and which was, and which is to come, the Almighty.

9 I John, who also am your brother, and companion in tribulation, and in the kingdom and patience of Jesus Christ, was in the isle that is called Patmos, for the word of God, and for the testimony of Jesus Christ.

John's Vision of Christ

10 I was in the Spirit on the Lord's day, and heard behind me a great voice, as of a trumpet,

11 Saying, I am Alpha and Omega, the first and the last: and, What thou seest, write in a book, and send [it] unto the seven churches which are in Asia; unto

Ephesus, and unto Smyrna, and unto Pergamos, and unto Thyatira, and unto Sardis, and unto Philadelphia, and unto Laodicea.

12 And I turned to see the voice that spake with me. And being turned, I saw seven golden candlesticks;

13 And in the midst of the seven candlesticks [one] like unto the Son of man, clothed with a garment down to the foot, and girt about the paps with a golden girdle.

14 His head and [his] hairs [were] white like wool, as white as snow; and his eyes [were] as a flame of fire;

15 And his feet like unto fine brass, as if they burned in a furnace; and his voice as the sound of many waters.

16 And he had in his right hand seven stars: and out of his mouth went a sharp two-edged sword: and his countenance [was] as the sun shineth in his strength. 17 And when I saw him, I fell at his feet as dead. And he laid his right hand upon me, saying unto me, Fear not; I am the first and the last:

18 I [am] he that liveth, and was dead; and, behold, I am alive for evermore, Amen; and have the keys of hell and of death.

19 Write the things which thou hast seen, and the things which are, and the things which shall be

hereafter;

20 The mystery of the seven stars which thou sawest in my right hand, and the seven golden candlesticks. The seven stars are the angels of the seven churches: and the seven candlesticks which thou sawest are the seven churches.

CHAPTER 2

1 Unto the angel of the church of Ephesus write; These things saith he that holdeth the seven stars in his right hand, who walketh in the midst of the seven golden candlesticks;

2 I know thy works, and thy labour, and thy patience, and how thou canst not bear them which are evil: and thou hast tried them which say they are apostles, and are not, and hast found them liars:

3 And hast borne, and hast patience, and for my name's sake hast laboured, and hast not fainted.

4 Nevertheless I have [somewhat] against thee, because thou hast left thy first love.

5 Remember therefore from whence thou art fallen, and repent, and do the first works; or else I will come unto thee quickly, and will remove thy candlestick out

of his place, except thou repent.

6 But this thou hast, that thou hatest the deeds of the Nicolaitans, which I also hate.

7 He that hath an ear, let him hear what the Spirit saith unto the churches; To him that overcometh will I give to eat of the tree of life, which is in the midst of the paradise of God.

8 And unto the angel of the church in Smyrna write; These things saith the first and the last, which was dead, and is alive;

9 I know thy works, and tribulation, and poverty, (but thou art rich) and [I know] the blasphemy of them which say they are Jews, and are not, but [are] the synagogue of Satan.

10 Fear none of those things which thou shalt suffer: behold, the devil shall cast [some] of you into prison, that ye may be tried; and ye shall have tribulation ten days: be thou faithful unto death, and I will give thee a crown of life.

11 He that hath an ear, let him hear what the Spirit saith unto the churches; He that overcometh shall not be hurt of the second death.

12 And to the angel of the church in Pergamos write;

These things saith he which hath the sharp sword with two edges;

13 I know thy works, and where thou dwellest, [even] where Satan's seat [is]: and thou holdest fast my name, and hast not denied my faith, even in those days wherein Antipas [was] my faithful martyr, who was slain among you, where Satan dwelleth.

14 But I have a few things against thee, because thou hast there them that hold the doctrine of Balaam, who taught Balac to cast a stumbling-block before the children of Israel, to eat things sacrificed unto idols, and to commit fornication.

15 So hast thou also them that hold the doctrine of the Nicolaitans, which thing I hate.

16 Repent; or else I will come unto thee quickly, and will fight against them with the sword of my mouth.

17 He that hath an ear, let him hear what the Spirit saith unto the churches; To him that overcometh will I give to eat of the hidden manna, and will give him a white stone, and in the stone a new name written, which no man knoweth saving he that receiveth [it].

18 And unto the angel of the church in Thyatira write; These things saith the Son of God, who hath his eyes

like unto a flame of fire, and his feet [are] like fine brass;

19 I know thy works, and charity, and service, and faith, and thy patience, and thy works; and the last [to be] more than the first.

20 Notwithstanding I have a few things against thee, because thou sufferest that woman Jezebel, which calleth herself a prophetess, to teach and to seduce my servants to commit fornication, and to eat things sacrificed unto idols.

21 And I gave her space to repent of her fornication; and she repented not.

22 Behold, I will cast her into a bed, and them that commit adultery with her into great tribulation, except they repent of their deeds.

23 And I will kill her children with death; and all the churches shall know that I am he which searcheth the reins and hearts: and I will give unto every one of you according to your works.

24 But unto you I say, and unto the rest in Thyatira, as many as have not this doctrine, and which have not known the depths of Satan, as they speak; I will put upon you none other burden.

25 But that which ye have [already] hold fast till I come.

26 And he that overcometh, and keepeth my works unto the end, to him will I give power over the nations:

27 And he shall rule them with a rod of iron; as the vessels of a potter shall they be broken to shivers: even as I received of my Father.

28 And I will give him the morning star.

29 He that hath an ear, let him hear what the Spirit saith unto the churches.

CHAPTER 3

1 And unto the angel of the church in Sardis write; These things saith he that hath the seven Spirits of God, and the seven stars; I know thy works, that thou hast a name that thou livest, and art dead.

2 Be watchful, and strengthen the things which remain, that are ready to die: for I have not found thy works perfect before God.

3 Remember therefore how thou hast received and

heard, and hold fast, and repent. If therefore thou shalt not watch, I will come on thee as a thief, and thou shalt not know what hour I will come upon thee.

4 Thou hast a few names even in Sardis which have not defiled their garments; and they shall walk with me in white: for they are worthy.

5 He that overcometh, the same shall be clothed in white raiment; and I will not blot out his name out of the book of life, but I will confess his name before my Father, and before his angels.

6 He that hath an ear, let him hear what the Spirit saith unto the churches.

7 And to the angel of the church in Philadelphia write; These things saith he that is holy, he that is true, he that hath the key of David, he that openeth, and no man shutteth; and shutteth, and no man openeth;

8 I know thy works: behold, I have set before thee an open door, and no man can shut it: for thou hast a little strength, and hast kept my word, and hast not denied my name.

9 Behold, I will make them of the synagogue of Satan, which say they are Jews, and are not, but do lie; behold, I will make them to come and worship before

thy feet, and to know that I have loved thee.

10Because thou hast kept the word of my patience, I also will keep thee from the hour of temptation, which shall come upon all the world, to try them that dwell upon the earth.

11 Behold, I come quickly: hold that fast which thou hast, that no man take thy crown.

12Him that overcometh will I make a pillar in the temple of my God, and he shall go no more out: and I will write upon him the name of my God and the name of the city of my God, [which is] new Jerusalem, which cometh down out of heaven from my God: and [I will write upon him] my new name.

13He that hath an ear, let him hear what the Spirit saith unto the churches.

14And unto the angel of the church of the Laodiceans write; These things saith the Amen, the faithful and true witness, the beginning of the creation of God;

15I know thy works, that thou art neither cold nor hot: I would thou wert cold or hot.

16So then because thou art lukewarm, and neither cold nor hot, I will spue thee out of my mouth.

17Because thou sayest, I am rich, and increased with

goods, and have need of nothing; and knowest not that thou art wretched, and miserable, and poor, and blind, and naked:

18I counsel thee to buy of me gold tried in the fire, that thou mayest be rich; and white raiment, that thou mayest be clothed, and [that] the shame of thy nakedness do not appear; and anoint thine eyes with eyesalve, that thou mayest see.

19 As many as I love, I rebuke and chasten: be zealous therefore, and repent.

20 Behold, I stand at the door, and knock: if any man hear my voice, and open the door, I will come in to him, and will sup with him, and he with me.

21To him that overcometh will I grant to sit with me in my throne, even as I also overcame, and am set down with my Father in his throne.

22 He that hath an ear, let him hear what the Spirit saith unto the churches.

CHAPTER 4

1 After this I looked, and, behold, a door [was] opened in heaven: and the first voice which I heard [was] as it

were of a trumpet talking with me; which said, Come up hither, and I will shew thee things which must be hereafter.

2 And immediately I was in the spirit: and, behold, a throne was set in heaven, and [one] sat on the throne.

3 And he that sat was to look upon like a jasper and a sardine stone: and [there was] a rainbow round about the throne, in sight like unto an emerald.

4 And round about the throne [were] four and twenty seats: and upon the seats I saw four and twenty elders sitting, clothed in white raiment; and they had on their heads crowns of gold.

5 And out of the throne proceeded lightnings and thunderings and voices: and [there were] seven lamps of fire burning before the throne, which are the seven Spirits of God.

6 And before the throne [there was] a sea of glass like unto crystal: and in the midst of the throne, and round about the throne, [were] four beasts full of eyes before and behind.

7 And the first beast [was] like a lion, and the second beast like a calf, and the third beast had a face as a man, and the fourth beast [was] like a flying eagle.

8 And the four beasts had each of them six wings about [him]; and [they were] full of eyes within: and they rest not day and night, saying, Holy, holy, holy, Lord God Almighty, which was, and is, and is to come.

9 And when those beasts give glory and honour and thanks to him that sat on the throne, who liveth for ever and ever,

10 The four and twenty elders fall down before him that sat on the throne, and worship him that liveth for ever and ever, and cast their crowns before the throne, saying,

11 Thou art worthy, O Lord, to receive glory and honour and power: for thou hast created all things, and for thy pleasure they are and were created.

CHAPTER 5

1 And I saw in the right hand of him that sat on the throne a book written within and on the backside, sealed with seven seals.

2 And I saw a strong angel proclaiming with a loud voice, Who is worthy to open the book, and to loose the seals thereof?

3 And no man in heaven, nor in earth, neither under

the earth, was able to open the book, neither to look thereon.

4 And I wept much, because no man was found worthy to open and to read the book, neither to look thereon.

5 And one of the elders saith unto me, Weep not: behold, the Lion of the tribe of Juda, the Root of David, hath prevailed to open the book, and to loose the seven seals thereof.

6 And I beheld, and, lo, in the midst of the throne and of the four beasts, and in the midst of the elders, stood a Lamb as it had been slain, having seven horns and seven eyes, which are the seven Spirits of God sent forth into all the earth.

7 And he came and took the book out of the right hand of him that sat upon the throne.

8 And when he had taken the book, the four beasts and four [and] twenty elders fell down before the Lamb, having every one of them harps, and golden vials full of odours, which are the prayers of saints.

9 And they sung a new song, saying, Thou art worthy to take the book, and to open the seals thereof: for thou wast slain, and hast redeemed us to God by thy

blood out of every kindred, and tongue, and people, and nation;

10 And hast made us unto our God kings and priests: and we shall reign on the earth.

11 And I beheld, and I heard the voice of many angels round about the throne and the beasts and the elders: and the number of them was ten thousand times ten thousand, and thousands of thousands;

12 Saying with a loud voice, Worthy is the Lamb that was slain to receive power, and riches, and wisdom, and strength, and honour, and glory, and blessing.

13 And every creature which is in heaven, and on the earth, and under the earth, and such as are in the sea, and all that are in them, heard I saying, Blessing, and honour, and glory, and power, [be] unto him that sitteth upon the throne, and unto the Lamb for ever and ever.

14 And the four beasts said, Amen. And the four [and] twenty elders fell down and worshipped him that liveth for ever and ever.

(Author's note: Below is the first portion of Scriptures that I have moved into chronological order. Note that I am placing the verses I move

into chronological order in bold so they will stand out, identifying that they have been moved. When you read Revelation chapters 12:1 – 13:2, realize that this portion of scripture is painting an unfolding picture of what will be happening leading up to the opening of the seals. Picture this information as an overlay of additional information that gives us a clearer picture of what is about to happen.)

The Woman and the Dragon

Rev. 12:1 – 13:2

1 And there appeared a great wonder in heaven; a woman clothed with the sun, and the moon under her feet, and upon her head a crown of twelve stars:

2 And she being with child cried, travailing in birth, and pained to be delivered.

3 And there appeared another wonder in heaven; and behold a great red dragon, having seven heads and ten horns, and seven crowns upon his heads.

4 And his tail drew the third part of the stars of heaven, and did cast them to the earth: and the dragon stood before the woman which was ready

to be delivered, for to devour her child as soon as it was born.

5 And she brought forth a man child, who was to rule all nations with a rod of iron: and her child was caught up unto God, and [to] his throne.

6 And the woman fled into the wilderness, where she hath a place prepared of God, that they should feed her there a thousand two hundred [and] threescore days.

7 And there was war in heaven: Michael and his angels fought against the dragon; and the dragon fought and his angels,

8 And prevailed not; neither was their place found any more in heaven.

9 And the great dragon was cast out, that old serpent, called the Devil, and Satan, which deceiveth the whole world: he was cast out into the earth, and his angels were cast out with him.

10 And I heard a loud voice saying in heaven, Now is come salvation, and strength, and the kingdom of our God, and the power of his Christ: for the accuser of our brethren is cast down, which accused them before our God day and night.

11 And they overcame him by the blood of the Lamb, and by the word of their testimony; and they loved not their lives unto the death.

12 Therefore rejoice, [ye] heavens, and ye that dwell in them. Woe to the inhabiters of the earth and of the sea! for the devil is come down unto you, having great wrath, because he knoweth that he hath but a short time.

13 And when the dragon saw that he was cast unto the earth, he persecuted the woman which brought forth the man [child].

14 And to the woman were given two wings of a great eagle, that she might fly into the wilderness, into her place, where she is nourished for a time, and times, and half a time, from the face of the serpent.

15 And the serpent cast out of his mouth water as a flood after the woman, that he might cause her to be carried away of the flood.

16 And the earth helped the woman, and the earth opened her mouth, and swallowed up the flood which the dragon cast out of his mouth.

17 And the dragon was wroth with the woman, and

went to make war with the remnant of her seed, which keep the commandments of God, and have the testimony of Jesus Christ.

CHAPTER 13

1 And I stood upon the sand of the sea, and saw a beast rise up out of the sea, having seven heads and ten horns, and upon his horns ten crowns, and upon his heads the name of blasphemy.

2 And the beast which I saw was like unto a leopard and his feet were as [the feet] of a bear, and his mouth as the mouth of a lion: and the dragon gave him his power, and his seat, and great authority.

The Opening of the Seals

Rev. 6:1 – 2

And I saw when the Lamb opened one of the seals, and I heard, as it were the noise of thunder, one of the four beasts saying, Come and see. 2

And I saw, and behold a white horse: and he that sat on him had a bow: and a crown was given unto him: and he went forth conquering, and to conquer.

Revelation 13:3-18

3 And I saw one of his heads as it were wounded to death; and his deadly wound was healed: and all the world wondered after the beast.

4 And they worshipped the dragon which gave power unto the beast: and they worshipped the beast, saying, Who [is] like unto the beast? who is able to make war with him?

5 And there was given unto him a mouth speaking great things and blasphemies; and power was given unto him to continue forty [and] two months.

6 And he opened his mouth in blasphemy against God, to blaspheme his name, and his tabernacle, and them that dwell in heaven.

7 And it was given unto him to make war with the saints, and to overcome them: and power was

given him over all kindreds, and tongues, and nations.

8 And all that dwell upon the earth shall worship him, whose names are not written in the book of life of the Lamb slain from the foundation of the world.

9 If any man have an ear, let him hear.

10 He that leadeth into captivity shall go into captivity: he that killeth with the sword must be killed with the sword. Here is the patience and the faith of the saints.

11 And I beheld another beast coming up out of the earth; and he had two horns like a lamb, and he spake as a dragon.

12 And he exerciseth all the power of the first beast before him, and causeth the earth and them which dwell therein to worship the first beast, whose deadly wound was healed.

13 And he doeth great wonders, so that he maketh fire come down from heaven on the earth in the sight of men,

14 And deceiveth them that dwell on the earth by

[the means of] those miracles which he had power to do in the sight of the beast; saying to them that dwell on the earth, that they should make an image to the beast, which had the wound by a sword, and did live.

15 And he had power to give life unto the image of the beast, that the image of the beast should both speak, and cause that as many as would not worship the image of the beast should be killed.

16 And he causeth all, both small and great, rich and poor, free and bond, to receive a mark in their right hand, or in their foreheads:

17 And that no man might buy or sell, save he that had the mark, or the name of the beast, or the number of his name.

18 Here is wisdom. Let him that hath understanding count the number of the beast: for it is the number of a man; and his number [is] Six hundred threescore [and] six.

The Three Angels

(Author's note: This next portion of Scripture that I am placing in chronological order. I am placing between the first and second seals because I see this time of the Tribulation as a time of great trial for the believers. This will be an hour of trial that will either drive the lukewarm Christians closer to God or away from God. God is sending His angels to preach the gospel at a time when the antichrist is trying to shut down the preaching of God's Word. The Rapture will happen before the Wrath of God begins, but this hour of judgment will be a time when God is calling his children back to a place of repentance as the Great Tribulation is getting underway.)

Rev. 14:6-7

6 And I saw another angel fly in the midst of heaven, having the everlasting gospel to preach unto them that dwell on the earth, and to every nation, and kindred, and tongue, and people,

7 Saying with a loud voice, Fear God, and give glory to him; for the hour of his judgment is come: and worship him that made heaven, and earth, and the sea, and the fountains of waters.

Rev. 6:3 – 7:8

3 And when he had opened the second seal, I heard the second beast say, Come and see.

4 And there went out another horse *that was* red: and *power* was given to him that sat thereon to take peace from the earth, and that they should kill one another: and there was given unto him a great sword.

5 And when he had opened the third seal, I heard the third beast say, Come and see. And I beheld, and lo a black horse; and he that sat on him had a pair of balances in his hand.

6 And I heard a voice in the midst of the four beasts say, A measure of wheat for a penny, and three measures of barley for a penny; and *see* thou hurt not the oil and the wine.

7 And when he had opened the fourth seal, I heard the voice of the fourth beast say, Come and see.

8 And I looked, and behold a pale horse: and his name that sat on him was Death, and Hell followed with him. And power was given unto them over the fourth part of the earth, to kill with sword, and with

hunger, and with death, and with the beasts of the earth.

9 And when he had opened the fifth seal, I saw under the altar the souls of them that were slain for the word of God, and for the testimony which they held:

10 And they cried with a loud voice, saying, How long, O Lord, holy and true, dost thou not judge and avenge our blood on them that dwell on the earth?

11 And white robes were given unto every one of them; and it was said unto them, that they should rest yet for a little season, until their fellowservants also and their brethren, that should be killed as they *were*, should be fulfilled.

12 And I beheld when he had opened the sixth seal, and, lo, there was a great earthquake; and the sun became black as sackcloth of hair, and the moon became as blood;

13 And the stars of heaven fell unto the earth, even as a fig tree casteth her untimely figs, when she is shaken of a mighty wind.

14 And the heaven departed as a scroll when it is rolled together; and every mountain and island

were moved out of their places.

15 And the kings of the earth, and the great men, and the rich men, and the chief captains, and the mighty men, and every bondman, and every free man, hid themselves in the dens and in the rocks of the mountains;

16 And said to the mountains and rocks, Fall on us, and hide us from the face of him that sitteth on the throne, and from the wrath of the Lamb:

17 For the great day of his wrath is come; and who shall be able to stand?

CHAPTER 7

1 And after these things I saw four angels standing on the four corners of the earth, holding the four winds of the earth, that the wind should not blow on the earth, nor on the sea, nor on any tree.

2 And I saw another angel ascending from the east, having the seal of the living God: and he cried with a loud voice to the four angels, to whom it was given to hurt the earth and the sea,

3 Saying, Hurt not the earth, neither the sea, nor the trees, till we have sealed the servants of our God

in their foreheads.

4 And I heard the number of them which were sealed: *and there were* sealed an hundred *and* forty *and* four thousand of all the tribes of the children of Israel.

5 Of the tribe of Juda *were* sealed twelve thousand. Of the tribe of Reuben *were* sealed twelve thousand. Of the tribe of Gad *were* sealed twelve thousand.

6 Of the tribe of Aser *were* sealed twelve thousand. Of the tribe of Nepthalim *were* sealed twelve thousand. Of the tribe of Manasses *were* sealed twelve thousand.

7 Of the tribe of Simeon *were* sealed twelve thousand. Of the tribe of Levi *were* sealed twelve thousand. Of the tribe of Issachar *were* sealed twelve thousand.

8 Of the tribe of Zabulon *were* sealed twelve thousand. Of the tribe of Joseph *were* sealed twelve thousand. Of the tribe of Benjamin *were* sealed twelve thousand.

(Author's note: Realize that Revelation chapter 11: 1-14 is describing the time of the two witnesses, a 3.5 year period that will start a short time before the rapture and extend to the time of their death just before the seventh bowl of God's wrath. Because the events from this overlay are spread over a three and a half year period it will seem that some events are happening too soon. Look at this portion of scripture as starting at this point in my timeline but at the same time it is giving future insights of things to happen over the 3.5 years covered in this section of Scripture.)

The Two Witnesses   Revelation 11: 1-14

1 And there was given me a reed like unto a rod: and the angel stood, saying, Rise, and measure the temple of God, and the altar, and them that worship therein.

2 But the court which is without the temple leave out, and measure it not; for it is given unto the Gentiles: and the holy city shall they tread under foot forty [and] two months.

3 And I will give [power] unto my two witnesses, and they shall prophesy a thousand two hundred [and] threescore days, clothed in sackcloth.

4 These are the two olive trees, and the two candlesticks standing before the God of the earth.

5 And if any man will hurt them, fire proceedeth

out of their mouth, and devoureth their enemies: and if any man will hurt them, he must in this manner be killed.

6 These have power to shut heaven, that it rain not in the days of their prophecy: and have power over waters to turn them to blood, and to smite the earth with all plagues, as often as they will.

7 And when they shall have finished their testimony, the beast that ascendeth out of the bottomless pit shall make war against them, and shall overcome them, and kill them.

8 And their dead bodies [shall lie] in the street of the great city, which spiritually is called Sodom and Egypt, where also our Lord was crucified.

9 And they of the people and kindreds and tongues and nations shall see their dead bodies three days and an half, and shall not suffer their dead bodies to be put in graves.

10 And they that dwell upon the earth shall rejoice over them, and make merry, and shall send gifts one to another; because these two prophets tormented them that dwelt on the earth.

11 And after three days and an half the Spirit of

life from God entered into them, and they stood upon their feet; and great fear fell upon them which saw them.

12 And they heard a great voice from heaven saying unto them, Come up hither. And they ascended up to heaven in a cloud; and their enemies beheld them.

13 And the same hour was there a great earthquake, and the tenth part of the city fell, and in the earthquake were slain of men seven thousand: and the remnant were affrighted, and gave glory to the God of heaven.

14 The second woe is past; [and], behold, the third woe cometh quickly.

(Author's note: The following portion of scripture showing the fall of Babylon, corresponds with Revelation 17 and 18, that describes the destruction of Mystery Babylon, with this study showing that this event happens before the rapture as seen in Revelation 7:9. You will note this verse describes the saints needed patience to endure this period of tribulation.)

Revelation 14:8-13

The Destruction of Mystery Babylon

8 And there followed another angel, saying, Babylon is fallen, is fallen, that great city, because she made all nations drink of the wine of the wrath of her fornication.

9 And the third angel followed them, saying with a loud voice, If any man worship the beast and his image, and receive [his] mark in his forehead, or in his hand,

10 The same shall drink of the wine of the wrath of God, which is poured out without mixture into the cup of his indignation; and he shall be tormented with fire and brimstone in the presence of the holy angels, and in the presence of the Lamb:

11 And the smoke of their torment ascendeth up for ever and ever: and they have no rest day nor night, who worship the beast and his image, and whosoever receiveth the mark of his name.

12 Here is the patience of the saints: here [are] they that keep the commandments of God, and the faith of Jesus.

13 And I heard a voice from heaven saying unto me, Write, Blessed [are] the dead which die in the

Lord from henceforth: Yea, saith the Spirit, that they may rest from their labours; and their works do follow them

(Author's note: Again the following portion of Scripture covering Revelation 17:1 – 19:10 is covering an extended period of time. These two and a half chapters cover the destruction of Mystery Babylon to the time of the Rapture and our arrival at the Throne, where it concludes with a proclamation that the time for the marriage of the Lamb to His bride has arrived. Look at this portion of Revelation as an overlay of information that gives further illumination to the Revelation that Jesus gave to John. Following this overlay of information will be further Scriptures pointing to the Rapture)

Babylon, the Prostitute on the Beast,

Revelation 17:1 - 19:10

1 And there came one of the seven angels which had the seven vials, and talked with me, saying unto me, Come hither; I will shew unto thee the judgment of the great whore that sitteth upon many waters:

2 With whom the kings of the earth have

committed fornication, and the inhabitants of the earth have been made drunk with the wine of her fornication.

3 So he carried me away in the spirit into the wilderness: and I saw a woman sit upon a scarlet coloured beast, full of names of blasphemy, having seven heads and ten horns.

4 And the woman was arrayed in purple and scarlet colour, and decked with gold and precious stones and pearls, having a golden cup in her hand full of abominations and filthiness of her fornication:

5 And upon her forehead [was] a name written, MYSTERY, BABYLON THE GREAT, THE MOTHER OF HARLOTS AND ABOMINATIONS OF THE EARTH.

6 And I saw the woman drunken with the blood of the saints, and with the blood of the martyrs of Jesus: and when I saw her, I wondered with great admiration.

7 And the angel said unto me, Wherefore didst thou marvel? I will tell thee the mystery of the woman, and of the beast that carrieth her, which

hath the seven heads and ten horns.

8 The beast that thou sawest was, and is not; and shall ascend out of the bottomless pit, and go into perdition: and they that dwell on the earth shall wonder, whose names were not written in the book of life from the foundation of the world, when they behold the beast that was, and is not, and yet is.

9 And here [is] the mind which hath wisdom. The seven heads are seven mountains, on which the woman sitteth.

10 And there are seven kings: five are fallen, and one is, [and] the other is not yet come; and when he cometh, he must continue a short space.

11 And the beast that was, and is not, even he is the eighth, and is of the seven, and goeth into perdition.

12 And the ten horns which thou sawest are ten kings, which have received no kingdom as yet; but receive power as kings one hour with the beast.

13 These have one mind, and shall give their power and strength unto the beast.

14 These shall make war with the Lamb, and the

Lamb shall overcome them: for he is Lord of lords, and King of kings: and they that are with him [are] called, and chosen, and faithful.

15 And he saith unto me, The waters which thou sawest, where the whore sitteth, are peoples, and multitudes, and nations, and tongues.

16 And the ten horns which thou sawest upon the beast, these shall hate the whore, and shall make her desolate and naked, and shall eat her flesh, and burn her with fire.

17 For God hath put in their hearts to fulfil his will, and to agree, and give their kingdom unto the beast, until the words of God shall be fulfilled.

18 And the woman which thou sawest is that great city, which reigneth over the kings of the earth.

CHAPTER 18

1 And after these things I saw another angel come down from heaven, having great power; and the earth was lightened with his glory.

2 And he cried mightily with a strong voice, saying, Babylon the great is fallen, is fallen, and is become the habitation of devils, and the hold of

every foul spirit, and a cage of every unclean and hateful bird.

3 For all nations have drunk of the wine of the wrath of her fornication, and the kings of the earth have committed fornication with her, and the merchants of the earth are waxed rich through the abundance of her delicacies.

4 And I heard another voice from heaven, saying, Come out of her, my people, that ye be not partakers of her sins, and that ye receive not of her plagues.

5 For her sins have reached unto heaven, and God hath remembered her iniquities.

6 Reward her even as she rewarded you, and double unto her double according to her works: in the cup which she hath filled fill to her double.

7 How much she hath glorified herself, and lived deliciously, so much torment and sorrow give her: for she saith in her heart, I sit a queen, and am no widow, and shall see no sorrow.

8 Therefore shall her plagues come in one day, death, and mourning, and famine; and she shall be utterly burned with fire: for strong [is] the

Lord God who judgeth her.

9 And the kings of the earth, who have committed fornication and lived deliciously with her, shall bewail her, and lament for her, when they shall see the smoke of her burning,

10 Standing afar off for the fear of her torment, saying, Alas, alas, that great city Babylon, that mighty city! for in one hour is thy judgment come.

11 And the merchants of the earth shall weep and mourn over her; for no man buyeth their merchandise any more:

12 The merchandise of gold, and silver, and precious stones, and of pearls, and fine linen, and purple, and silk, and scarlet, and all thyine wood, and all manner vessels of ivory, and all manner vessels of most precious wood, and of brass, and iron, and marble,

13 And cinnamon, and odours, and ointments, and frankincense, and wine, and oil, and fine flour, and wheat, and beasts, and sheep, and horses, and chariots, and slaves, and souls of men.

14 And the fruits that thy soul lusted after are departed from thee, and all things which were

dainty and goodly are departed from thee, and thou shalt find them no more at all.

15 The merchants of these things, which were made rich by her, shall stand afar off for the fear of her torment, weeping and wailing,

16 And saying, Alas, alas, that great city, that was clothed in fine linen, and purple, and scarlet, and decked with gold, and precious stones, and pearls!

17 For in one hour so great riches is come to nought. And every shipmaster, and all the company in ships, and sailors, and as many as trade by sea, stood afar off,

18 And cried when they saw the smoke of her burning, saying, What [city is] like unto this great city!

19 And they cast dust on their heads, and cried, weeping and wailing, saying, Alas, alas, that great city, wherein were made rich all that had ships in the sea by reason of her costliness! for in one hour is she made desolate.

20 Rejoice over her, [thou] heaven, and [ye] holy apostles and prophets; for God hath avenged you

on her.

21 And a mighty angel took up a stone like a great millstone, and cast [it] into the sea, saying, Thus with violence shall that great city Babylon be thrown down, and shall be found no more at all.

22 And the voice of harpers, and musicians, and of pipers, and trumpeters, shall be heard no more at all in thee; and no craftsman, of whatsoever craft [he be], shall be found any more in thee; and the sound of a millstone shall be heard no more at all in thee;

23 And the light of a candle shall shine no more at all in thee; and the voice of the bridegroom and of the bride shall be heard no more at all in thee: for thy merchants were the great men of the earth; for by thy sorceries were all nations deceived.

24 And in her was found the blood of prophets, and of saints, and of all that were slain upon the earth.

CHAPTER 19

1 And after these things I heard a great voice of much people in heaven, saying, Alleluia; Salvation, and glory, and honour, and power, unto

the Lord our God:

2 For true and righteous [are] his judgments: for he hath judged the great whore, which did corrupt the earth with her fornication, and hath avenged the blood of his servants at her hand.

3 And again they said, Alleluia. And her smoke rose up for ever and ever.

4 And the four and twenty elders and the four beasts fell down and worshipped God that sat on the throne, saying, Amen; Alleluia.

5 And a voice came out of the throne, saying, Praise our God, all ye his servants, and ye that fear him, both small and great.

6 And I heard as it were the voice of a great multitude, and as the voice of many waters, and as the voice of mighty thunderings, saying, Alleluia: for the Lord God omnipotent reigneth.

7 Let us be glad and rejoice, and give honour to him: for the marriage of the Lamb is come, and his wife hath made herself ready.

8 And to her was granted that she should be arrayed in fine linen, clean and white: for the fine linen is the righteousness of saints.

9 And he saith unto me, Write, Blessed [are] they which are called unto the marriage supper of the Lamb. And he saith unto me, These are the true sayings of God.

10 And I fell at his feet to worship him. And he said unto me, See [thou do it] not: I am thy fellow servant, and of thy brethren that have the testimony of Jesus: worship God: for the testimony of Jesus is the spirit of prophecy.

Revelation 14:14-16

Harvesting the Earth and Trampling the Winepress

14 And I looked, and behold a white cloud, and upon the cloud [one] sat like unto the Son of man, having on his head a golden crown, and in his hand a sharp sickle.

15 And another angel came out of the temple, crying with a loud voice to him that sat on the cloud, Thrust in thy sickle, and reap: for the time is come for thee to reap; for the harvest of the earth is ripe.

16 And he that sat on the cloud thrust in his sickle on the earth; and the earth was reaped.

The Great Multitude in White Robes

Revelation 7:9 – 8:1

9 After this I beheld, and, lo, a great multitude, which no man could number, of all nations, and kindreds, and people, and tongues, stood before the throne, and before the Lamb, clothed with white robes, and palms in their hands;

10 And cried with a loud voice, saying, Salvation to our God which sitteth upon the throne, and unto the Lamb.

11 And all the angels stood round about the throne, and [about] the elders and the four beasts, and fell before the throne on their faces, and worshipped God,

12 Saying, Amen: Blessing, and glory, and wisdom, and thanksgiving, and honour, and power, and might, [be] unto our God for ever and ever. Amen.

13 And one of the elders answered, saying unto

me, What are these which are arrayed in white robes? and whence came they?

14 And I said unto him, Sir, thou knowest. And he said to me, These are they which came out of great tribulation, and have washed their robes, and made them white in the blood of the Lamb.

15 Therefore are they before the throne of God, and serve him day and night in his temple: and he that sitteth on the throne shall dwell among them.

16 They shall hunger no more, neither thirst anymore; neither shall the sun light on them, nor any heat.

17 For the Lamb which is in the midst of the throne shall feed them, and shall lead them unto living fountains of waters: and God shall wipe away all tears from their eyes.

CHAPTER 8

1 And when he had opened the seventh seal, there was silence in heaven about the space of half an hour.

(Author's note: This portion of scripture that is moved to this location is covered in my earlier teaching in this study. Explaining the reasoning for moving these verses to this location. You will notice as you read this that both chapter 7 and 11 are taking place at the throne with the elders having a major role in there verses. The time frame for these verses extends into the beginning of the blowing of the seven trumpets of God's wrath.)

Revelation 11:16-19

16 And the four and twenty elders, which sat before God on their seats, fell upon their faces, and worshipped God,

17 Saying, We give thee thanks, O Lord God Almighty, which art, and wast, and art to come; because thou hast taken to thee thy great power, and hast reigned.

18 And the nations were angry, and thy wrath is come, and the time of the dead, that they should be judged, and that thou shouldest give reward unto thy servants the prophets, and to the saints, and them that fear thy name, small

and great; and shouldest destroy them which destroy the earth.

19 And the temple of God was opened in heaven, and there was seen in his temple the ark of his testament: and there were lightnings, and voices, and thunderings, and an earthquake, and great hail.

Revelation 8:2-10:11

2 And I saw the seven angels which stood before God; and to them were given seven trumpets.

3 And another angel came and stood at the altar, having a golden censer; and there was given unto

him much incense, that he should offer [it] with the prayers of all saints upon the golden altar which was before the throne.

4 And the smoke of the incense, [which came] with the prayers of the saints, ascended up before God out of the angel's hand.

5 And the angel took the censer, and filled

it with fire of the altar, and cast [it] into the earth: and there were voices, and thunderings, and lightnings, and an earthquake.

6 And the seven angels which had the seven trumpets prepared themselves to sound.

7 The first angel sounded, and there followed hail and fire mingled with blood, and they were cast upon the earth: and the third part of trees was burnt up, and all green grass was burnt up.

8 And the second angel sounded, and as it were a great mountain burning with fire was cast into the sea: and the third part of the sea became blood;

9 And the third part of the creatures which were in the sea, and had life, died; and the third part of the ships were destroyed.

10 And the third angel sounded, and there fell a great star from heaven, burning as it were a lamp, and it fell upon the third part of the rivers, and upon the fountains of waters;

11 And the name of the star is called Wormwood: and the third part of the waters became wormwood; and many men died of the waters, because they were made bitter.

12 And the fourth angel sounded, and the third part of the sun was smitten, and the third part of the moon, and the third part of the stars; so as the third part of them was darkened, and the day shone not for a third part of it, and the night likewise.

13 And I beheld, and heard an angel flying through the midst of heaven, saying with a loud voice, Woe, woe, woe, to the inhabiters of the earth by reason of the

other voices of the trumpet of the three angels, which are yet to sound!

CHAPTER 9

1 And the fifth angel sounded, and I saw a star fall from heaven unto the earth: and to him was given the key of the bottomless pit.

2 And he opened the bottomless pit; and there arose a smoke out of the pit, as the smoke of a

great furnace; and the sun and the air were darkened by reason of the smoke of the pit.

3 And there came out of the smoke locusts upon the earth: and unto them was given power, as the scorpions of the earth have power.

4 And it was commanded them that they should not hurt the grass of the earth, neither any green thing, neither any tree; but only those men which have not the seal of God in their foreheads.

5 And to them it was given that they should not kill them, but that they should be tormented five months: and their torment [was] as the torment of a scorpion, when he striketh a man.

6 And in those days shall men seek death, and shall not find it; and shall desire to die, and death shall flee from them.

7 And the shapes of the locusts [were] like unto horses prepared unto battle; and on their heads [were] as it were crowns like gold, and their faces [were] as the faces of men.

8 And they had hair as the hair of women, and their teeth were as [the teeth] of lions.

9 And they had breastplates, as it were breastplates of iron; and the sound of their wings [was] as the sound of chariots of many horses running to battle.

10 And they had tails like unto scorpions, and there were stings in their tails: and their power [was] to hurt men five months.

11 And they had a king over them, [which is] the angel of the bottomless pit, whose name in the Hebrew tongue [is] Abaddon, but in the Greek tongue hath [his] name Apollyon.

12 One woe is past; [and], behold, there come two woes more hereafter.

13 And the sixth angel sounded, and I heard a voice from the four horns of the golden altar which is before God,

14 Saying to the sixth angel which had the trumpet, Loose the four angels which are bound in the great river Euphrates.

15 And the four angels were loosed, which were prepared for an hour, and a day, and a month, and a year, for to slay the third part of men.

16 And the number of the army of the horsemen

[were] two hundred thousand thousand: and I heard the number of them.

17 And thus I saw the horses in the vision, and them that sat on them, having breastplates of fire, and of jacinth, and brimstone: and the heads of the horses [were] as the heads of lions; and out of their mouths issued fire and smoke and brimstone.

18 By these three was the third part of men killed, by the fire, and by the smoke, and by the brimstone, which issued out of their mouths.

19 For their power is in their mouth, and in their tails: for their tails [were] like unto serpents, and had heads, and with them they do hurt.

20 And the rest of the men which were not killed by these plagues yet repented not of the works of their hands, that they should not worship devils, and idols of gold, and silver, and brass, and stone, and of wood: which neither can see, nor hear, nor walk:

21 Neither repented they of their murders, nor of their sorceries, nor of their fornication, nor of their thefts.

(Author's note: The following portion of Scripture that has the instructions that the angel gave to John when John was interrupted by the angel. This portion is mostly showing how John came to have the little scroll that would contain new revelation that was added to what John was writing. This interruption gave John, Revelation chapters 11-14 that I have placed as foot notes in a chronological sequence in the Book of Revelation.)

The Angel and the Little Scroll

CHAPTER 10

1 And I saw another mighty angel come down from heaven, clothed with a cloud: and a rainbow [was] upon his head, and his face [was] as it were the sun, and his feet as pillars of fire:

2 And he had in his hand a little book open: and he set his right foot upon the sea, and [his] left [foot] on the earth,

3 And cried with a loud voice, as [when] a lion roareth: and when he had cried, seven thunders uttered their voices.

4 And when the seven thunders had uttered their voices, I was about to write: and I heard a voice from heaven saying unto me, Seal up those things

which the seven thunders uttered, and write them not.

5 And the angel which I saw stand upon the sea and upon the earth lifted up his hand to heaven,

6 And sware by him that liveth for ever and ever, who

created heaven, and the things that therein are,

and the earth, and the things that therein are,

and the sea and the things which are therein, that

there should be time no longer:

7 But in the days of the voice of the seventh angel, when he shall begin to sound, the mystery of God should be finished, as he hath declared to his servants the prophets.

8 And the voice which I heard from heaven spake unto me again, and said, Go [and] take the little book which is open in the hand of the angel which standeth upon the sea and upon the earth.

9 And I went unto the angel, and said unto him, Give me the little book. And he said unto me, Take [it], and eat it up; and it shall make thy belly bitter, but it shall be in thy mouth sweet as honey.

10 And I took the little book out of the angel's hand, and ate it up; and it was in my mouth sweet as honey: and as soon as I had eaten it, my belly was bitter.

11 And he said unto me, Thou must prophesy again before many peoples, and nations, and tongues, and kings.

(Author's note: This next verse covers the seventh trumpet, I see this as the middle of the wrath of God, the Rapture has already happened and events are happening in heaven while at the same time the full pressure of the wrath of God is being released on unrepentant man.)

The Seventh Trumpet

Revelation 11:15

And the seventh angel sounded; and there were great voices in heaven, saying,

The kingdoms of this world are become [the kingdoms] of our Lord, and of his Christ; and he shall reign for ever and ever.

(Author's note: We are about to read about the seven bowls of God's wrath. They are called the seven plaques. There are some who teach that these are the total of God's wrath. If you will read this next sentence you will see these bowls are called "the seven last plagues" they cannot be the last, unless there were others before them.)

Seven Angels with Seven Plagues

Revelation 15:1 – 16:21

1 And I saw another sign in heaven, great and marvellous, seven angels having the seven last plagues; for in them is filled up the wrath of God.

2 And I saw as it were a sea of glass mingled with fire: and them that had gotten the victory over the beast, and over his image, and over his mark, [and] over the number of his name, stand on the sea of glass, having the harps of God.

3 And they sing the song of Moses the servant of God, and the song of the Lamb, saying, Great and marvellous [are] thy works, Lord God Almighty; just and true [are] thy ways, thou King of saints.

4 Who shall not fear thee, O Lord, and glorify thy name? for [thou] only [art] holy: for all nations shall come and worship before thee; for thy judgments are made manifest.

5 And after that I looked, and, behold, the temple of the tabernacle of the testimony in heaven was opened:

6 And the seven angels came out of the temple, having the seven plagues, clothed in pure and white linen, and having their breasts girded with golden girdles.

7 And one of the four beasts gave unto the seven angels seven golden vials full of the wrath of God, who liveth for ever and ever.

8 And the temple was filled with smoke from the glory of God, and from his power; and no man was able to enter into the temple, till the seven plagues of the seven angels were fulfilled.

CHAPTER 16

1 And I heard a great voice out of the temple saying to the seven angels, Go your ways, and pour out the vials of the wrath of God upon the earth.

2 And the first went, and poured out his vial upon the earth; and there fell a noisome and grievous sore upon the men which had the mark of the

beast, and [upon] them which worshipped his image.

3 And the second angel poured out his vial upon the sea; and it became as the blood of a dead [man]: and every living soul died in the sea.

4 And the third angel poured out his vial upon the rivers and fountains of waters; and they became blood.

5 And I heard the angel of the waters say, Thou art righteous, O Lord, which art, and wast, and shalt be, because thou hast judged thus.

6 For they have shed the blood of saints and prophets, and thou hast given them blood to drink; for they are worthy.

7 And I heard another out of the altar say, Even so, Lord God Almighty, true and righteous [are] thy judgments.

8 And the fourth angel poured out his vial upon the sun; and power was given unto him to scorch men with fire.

9 And men were scorched with great heat, and blasphemed the name of God, which hath power over these plagues: and they repented not to give

him glory.

10 And the fifth angel poured out his vial upon the seat of the beast; and his kingdom was full of darkness; and they gnawed their tongues for pain,

11 And blasphemed the God of heaven because of their pains and their sores, and repented not of their deeds.

12 And the sixth angel poured out his vial upon the great river Euphrates; and the water thereof was dried up, that the way of the kings of the east might be prepared.

13 And I saw three unclean spirits like frogs [come] out of the mouth of the dragon, and out of the mouth of the beast, and out of the mouth of the false prophet.

14 For they are the spirits of devils, working miracles, [which] go forth unto the kings of the earth and of the whole world, to gather them to the battle of that great day of God Almighty.

15 Behold, I come as a thief. Blessed [is] he that watcheth, and keepeth his garments, lest he walk naked, and they see his shame.

16 And he gathered them together into a place

called in the Hebrew tongue Armageddon.

17 And the seventh angel poured out his vial into the air; and there came a great voice out of the temple of heaven, from the throne, saying, It is done.

18 And there were voices, and thunders, and lightnings; and there was a great earthquake, such as was not since men were upon the earth, so mighty an earthquake, [and] so great.

19 And the great city was divided into three parts, and the cities of the nations fell: and great Babylon came in remembrance before God, to give unto her the cup of the wine of the fierceness of his wrath.

20 And every island fled away, and the mountains were not found.

21 And there fell upon men a great hail out of heaven, [every stone] about the weight of a talent and men blasphemed God because of the plague of the hail; for the plague thereof was exceeding great.

Revelation 19:11 – 19:16

The Heavenly Warrior Defeats the Beast

11 And I saw heaven opened, and behold a white horse; and he that sat upon him [was] called Faithful and True, and in righteousness he doth judge and make war.

12 His eyes [were] as a flame of fire, and on his head [were] many crowns; and he had a name written, that no man knew, but he himself.

13 And he [was] clothed with a vesture dipped in blood: and his name is called The Word of God.

14 And the armies [which were] in heaven followed him upon white horses, clothed in fine linen, white and clean.

15 And out of his mouth goeth a sharp sword, that with it he should smite the nations: and he shall rule them with a rod of iron: and he treadeth the winepress of the fierceness and wrath of Almighty God.

16 And he hath on [his] vesture and on his thigh a name written, KING OF Kings, AND

LORD OF Lords.

(Author's note: The following Scripture portion references the Battle of Armageddon, as seen where it says the blood flowed to the horses bridle.)

Revelation 14:17-20

17 And another angel came out of the temple which is in heaven, he also having a sharp sickle.

18 And another angel came out from the altar, which had power over fire; and cried with a loud cry to him that had the sharp sickle, saying, Thrust in thy sharp sickle, and gather the clusters of the vine of the earth; for her grapes are fully ripe.

19 And the angel thrust in his sickle into the earth, and gathered the vine of the earth, and cast [it] into the great winepress of the wrath of God.

20 And the winepress was trodden without the city, and blood came out of the winepress, even unto the horse bridles, by the space of a thousand [and] six hundred furlongs.

Revelation 19:17-20:3

17 And I saw an angel standing in the sun;

and he cried with a loud voice, saying to all the fowls that fly in the midst of heaven, Come and gather yourselves together unto the supper of the great God; 18 That ye may eat the flesh of kings, and the flesh of captains, and the flesh of mighty men, and the flesh of horses, and of them that sit on them, and the flesh of all [men, both] free and bond, both small and great. 19 And I saw the beast, and the kings of the earth, and their armies, gathered together to make war against him that sat on the horse, and against his army.

20And the beast was taken, and with him the false prophet that wrought miracles before him, with which he deceived them that had received the mark of the beast, and them that worshipped his image. These both were cast alive into a lake of fire burning with brimstone. 21 And the remnant were slain with the sword of him that sat upon the horse, which [sword] proceeded out of his mouth: and all the fowls were filled with their flesh.

The Thousand Years

1 And I saw an angel come down from heaven, having the key of the bottomless pit and a great chain in his hand.

2 And he laid hold on the dragon, that old serpent, which is the Devil, and Satan, and bound him a thousand years,

3 And cast him into the bottomless pit, and shut him up, and set a seal upon him, that he should deceive the nations no more, till the thousand years should be fulfilled: and after that he must be loosed a little season.

(Author's note: The following verses are where I pointed out earlier, that Jesus meets with the 144,000 after the Battle of Armageddon. This verse is the transition where Jesus meets with the 144,000 on Mount Zion and this meeting transitions to the throne in heaven.)

Revelation 14: 1-5 , The Lamb and the 144,000,

1 And I looked, and, lo, a Lamb stood on the Mount Zion, and with him an hundred forty [and]

four thousand, having his Father's name written in their foreheads.

2 And I heard a voice from heaven, as the voice of many waters, and as the voice of a great thunder: and I heard the voice of harpers harping with their harps:

3 And they sung as it were a new song before the throne, and before the four beasts, and the elders: and no man could learn that song but the hundred [and] forty [and] four thousand, which were redeemed from the earth.

4 These are they which were not defiled with women; for they are virgins. These are they which follow the Lamb whithersoever he goeth. These were redeemed from among men, [being] the firstfruits unto God and to the Lamb.

5 And in their mouth was found no guile: for they are without fault before the throne of God.

Revelation 20:4 – 22:21

4 And I saw thrones, and they sat upon them, and judgment was given unto them: and [I saw]

the souls of them that were beheaded for the witness of Jesus, and for the word of God, and which had not worshipped the beast, neither his image, neither had received [his] mark upon their foreheads, or in their hands; and they lived and reigned with Christ a thousand years.

5 But the rest of the dead lived not again until the thousand years were finished. This [is] the first resurrection.

6 Blessed and holy [is] he that hath part in the first resurrection: on such the second death hath no power, but they shall be priests of God and of Christ, and shall reign with him a thousand years.

The Judgment of Satan

7 And when the thousand years are expired, Satan shall be loosed out of his prison,

8 And shall go out to deceive the nations which are in the four quarters of the earth, Gog and Magog, to gather them together to battle: the number of whom [is] as the sand of the sea.

9 And they went up on the breadth of the earth,

and compassed the camp of the saints about, and the beloved city: and fire came down from God out of heaven, and devoured them.

10 And the devil that deceived them was cast into the lake of fire and brimstone, where the beast and the false prophet [are], and shall be tormented day and night for ever and ever.

The Judgment of the Dead

11 And I saw a great white throne, and him that sat on it, from whose face the earth and the heaven fled away; and there was found no place for them.

12 And I saw the dead, small and great, stand before God; and the books were opened: and another book was opened, which is [the book] of life: and the dead were judged out of those things which were written in the books, according to their works.

13 And the sea gave up the dead which were in it; and death and hell delivered up the dead which were in them: and they were judged

every man according to their works.

14 And death and hell were cast into the lake of fire. This is the second death.

15 And whosoever was not found written in the book of life was cast into the lake of fire.

Revelation 21:1-27

A New Heaven and a New Earth

1 And I saw a new heaven and a new earth: for the first heaven and the first earth were passed away; and there was no more sea.

2 And I John saw the holy city, new Jerusalem, coming down from God out of heaven, prepared as a bride adorned for her husband.

3 And I heard a great voice out of heaven saying, Behold, the tabernacle of God [is] with men, and he will dwell with them, and they shall be his people, and God himself shall be with them, [and be] their God.

4 And God shall wipe away all tears from their eyes; and there shall be no more death, neither sorrow, nor crying, neither shall there be any

more pain: for the former things are passed away.

5 And he that sat upon the throne said, Behold, I make all things new. And he said unto me, Write: for these words are true and faithful.

6 And he said unto me, It is done. I am Alpha and Omega, the beginning and the end. I will give unto him that is athirst of the fountain of the water of life freely.

7 He that overcometh shall inherit all things; and I will be his God, and he shall be my son.

8 But the fearful, and unbelieving, and the abominable, and murderers, and whoremongers, and sorcerers, and idolaters, and all liars, shall have their part in the lake which burneth with fire and brimstone: which is the second death.

The New Jerusalem, the Bride of the Lamb

9 And there came unto me one of the seven angels which had the seven vials full of the seven last plagues, and talked with me, saying, Come hither, I will shew thee the bride, the Lamb's

wife.

10 And he carried me away in the spirit to a great and high mountain, and shewed me that great city, the holy Jerusalem, descending out of heaven from God,

11 Having the glory of God: and her light [was] like unto a stone most precious, even like a jasper stone, clear as crystal;

12 And had a wall great and high, [and] had twelve gates, and at the gates twelve angels, and names written thereon, which are [the names] of the twelve tribes of the children of Israel:

13 On the east three gates; on the north three gates; on the south three gates; and on the west three gates.

14 And the wall of the city had twelve foundations, and in them the names of the twelve apostles of the Lamb.

15 And he that talked with me had a golden reed to measure the city, and the gates thereof, and the wall thereof.

16 And the city lieth foursquare, and the length is as large as the breadth: and he measured the

city with the reed, twelve thousand furlongs. The length and the breadth and the height of it are equal.

17 And he measured the wall thereof, an hundred [and] forty [and] four cubits, [according to] the measure of a man, that is, of the angel.

18 And the building of the wall of it was [of] jasper: and the city [was] pure gold, like unto clear glass.

19 And the foundations of the wall of the city [were] garnished with all manner of precious stones. The first

foundation was jasper; the second, sapphire;

the t h i r d , a chalcedony; the fourth, an emerald;

20 The fifth, sardonyx; the sixth, sardius; the seventh, chrysolite; the eighth, beryl; the ninth, a topaz; the tenth, a chrysoprasus; the eleventh, a jacinth; the twelfth, an amethyst.

21 And the twelve gates [were] twelve pearls; every several gate was of one pearl: and the street of the city [was] pure gold, as it were transparent glass.

22 And I saw no temple therein: for the Lord

God Almighty and the Lamb are the temple of it.

23 And the city had no need of the sun, neither of the moon, to shine in it: for the glory of God did lighten it, and the Lamb [is] the light thereof.

24 And the nations of them which are saved shall walk in the light of it: and the kings of the earth do bring their glory and honour into it.

25 And the gates of it shall not be shut at all by day: for there shall be no night there.

26 And they shall bring the glory and honour of the nations into it.

27 And there shall in no wise enter into it anything that defileth, neither [whatsoever] worketh abomination, or [maketh] a lie: but they which are written in the Lamb's book of life.

CHAPTER 22

1 And he shewed me a pure river of water of life, clear as crystal, proceeding out of the throne of God and of the Lamb.

2 In the midst of the street of it, and on either side of the river, [was there] the tree of life, which bare twelve [manner of] fruits, [and] yielded her

fruit every month: and the leaves of the tree [were] for the healing of the nations.

3 And there shall be no more curse: but the throne of God and of the Lamb shall be in it; and his servants shall serve him:

4 And they shall see his face; and his name [shall be] in their foreheads.

5 And there shall be no night there; and they need no candle, neither light of the sun; for the Lord God giveth them light: and they shall reign for ever and ever.

6 And he said unto me, These sayings [are] faithful and true: and the Lord God of the holy prophets sent his angel to shew unto his servants the things which must shortly be done.

7 Behold, I come quickly: blessed [is] he that keepeth the sayings of the prophecy of this book.

8 And I John saw these things, and heard [them]. And when I had heard and seen, I fell down to worship before the feet of the angel which shewed me these things.

9 Then saith he unto me, See [thou do it] not: for I am thy fellow servant, and of thy brethren the

prophets, and of them which keep the sayings of this book: worship God.

10 And he saith unto me, Seal not the sayings of the prophecy of this book: for the time is at hand.

11 He that is unjust, let him be unjust still: and he which is filthy, let him be filthy still: and he that is righteous, let him be righteous still: and he that is holy, let him be holy still.

12 And, behold, I come quickly; and my reward [is] with me, to give every man according as his work shall be.

13 I am Alpha and Omega, the beginning and the end, the first and the last.

14 Blessed [are] they that do his commandments, that they may have right to the tree of life, and may enter in through the gates into the city.

15 For without [are] dogs, and sorcerers, and whoremongers, and murderers, and idolaters, and whosoever loveth and maketh a lie.

16 I Jesus have sent mine angel to testify unto you these things in the churches. I am the root and the offspring of David, [and] the bright and morning star. 17 And the Spirit and the bride say,

Come. And let him that heareth say, Come. And let him that is athirst come. And whosoever will, let him take the water of life freely.

18 For I testify unto every man that heareth the words of the prophecy of this book, If any man shall add unto these things, God shall add unto him the plagues that are written in this book:

19 And if any man shall take away from the words of   the book of this prophecy, God shall take away his

part out of the book of life, and out of the holy city, and   [from] the things which are written in this book.

20 He which testifieth these things saith, Surely I come quickly. Amen. Even so, come, Lord Jesus.

21 The grace of our Lord Jesus Christ [be] with you all. Amen

The End

Understanding the Order of End Time Events

When Paul was brought to heaven and given great revelations by Jesus Christ, he was not sure if he was there in spirit or in body. Either way, what God revealed to Paul was an incredible revelation. When Daniel had his dream for the last days, he knew he had to write it down. I imagine Daniel was scrambling to get paper and pen to write down what he knew was an important revelation from God. Then John the Apostle, who was in prison on the island of Patmos, and was either taken to the throne in heaven or saw a vision of this event while in the spirit on the Lord's Day; it really does not matter which. When John was standing before Jesus, what an experience this must have been. When this vision was over, this is how I imagine the book of Revelation was written.

John arrives back home to reality. His heart and mind contain a great revelation of the Last Days. John knows this revelation is for the seven churches, basically for the whole body of Christ. John knows that he must write this message down. He is still in prison on the island of Patmos, probably not in a jail cell but some type of shelter, and he does not have paper (parchments) and pen just lying around. He makes contact with friends, and they smuggle these items in to him. Later, they will smuggle John's writings out. He sets himself to write down all that Jesus revealed to him. As he was writing, he was well into what we now know as the 10th chapter of the book of Revelation. Then an angel appears to John with additional revelation. What this angel shared with him was added to his writing assignment. This revelation was not placed in his writings with concern for being in chronological order but written in the order and timing of when it was given.

John then continues to write where he left off before being interrupted. When John finishes what we now know is chapter 16, which contains the final bowls of God's wrath, John is interrupted by an angel for a second time, (Revelation 17:1). Again John inserts this further revelation into the revelation that Jesus has shared with him. Then John continues where he left off, and he completes what we now know as the Book of Revelation.

I see that what John was given by the angel as additional footnotes to further illuminate what will happen in the Last Days. These footnotes are almost like additional pieces of a puzzle that we have not understood. Both Daniel and John were given revelation of what would happen in the last days, and they were both told that much of this revelation would remain a mystery until the time of the end. There is no doubt in my heart and my mind that we are now in the Last Days before Jesus Christ returns. I believe now is the time that God is removing the veil for us to see what is to soon come in these days.

What I will be doing now is reviewing this study and look at the order of future revelation events as shown from reading the book of Revelation in chronological order. I will then write a commentary on the highlights of the book of Revelation based on seeing the flow of events as shown in this study. I will not be expounding on every chapter and verse. I will be starting at the opening of the seals in Revelation chapter five. This will basically be a Bible study to help you see the coming revelation events more clearly and to help inspire you to do further study in what I believe is the most important book in the Bible in these last days.

Revelation chapter 5 contains what I see as the first prophetic event being described. Building up to the opening of the seals, Revelation 5:11-12 describes a great celebration happening around the throne as the seals are about to be opened. Notice these verses do not mention the saints in white robes around the throne at this time; an indication that the rapture has not happened yet. Revelation 5: 11-12 (KJV) *"And I beheld, and I heard the voice of many angels round about the throne and the beasts and the elders: and the number of them was ten thousand times ten thousand, and thousands of thousands; Saying with a loud voice, Worthy is the Lamb that was slain to receive power, and riches, and wisdom, and strength, and honor, and glory, and blessing."*

This next portion of the book of Revelation when read in chronological order jumps ahead to Revelation 12:1-13:2. These verses cover both past and future events that include the birth of Christ, Satan being cast to the earth and the coming one world government. One of the events described that has significance to the last days is found in Revelation 12:7-9. This is where we see Michael the archangel commanding the armies of God, fighting Satan and the fallen angels. This is when Satan and his fallen angels are defeated in the realm of heaven and cast to the earth. Satan is now no longer able to bring accusations to our heavenly Father against us.

Revelation 12: 7-10 (KJV) *"And there was war in heaven: Michael and his angels fought against the dragon; and the dragon fought and his angels, and prevailed not; neither was their place found any more in heaven. And the great dragon was cast out, that old serpent, called the devil, and Satan, which deceiveth the whole world: he was cast out into the earth, and his angels were cast out with him. And I heard a loud voice saying in heaven, Now is come salvation, and strength, and the kingdom of our God, and the power of his Christ: for the accuser of our brethren is cast down, which accused them before our God day and night."*

Revelation 12:12b describes the anger Satan will have after being cast to the earth. Revelation 12:12b (KJV) *"Woe to the inhibiters of the earth and the sea! for the devil is come down unto you, having great wrath, because he knoweth that he hath but a short time."*

Revelation 12:7 describes the beginning of Satan's wrath to be taken out against God's people. Daniel 7:25 describes Satan being given the liberty to make war on the saints for three and a half years. This leads to the anger of Satan as shown in Revelation 12:17 (KJV) *"And the dragon was wroth with the woman, and went to make war with the remnant of her seed, which keep the commandments of God, and have the testimony of Jesus Christ."* Revelation 13:1 describes the coming beast government being formed. Revelation 13:1 (KJV) *"And I stood upon the sand of the sea, and saw a beast rise up out of the sea, having seven heads and ten horns, and upon his horns ten crowns, and upon his heads the name of blasphemy."*

In my book, The Window of the Lord's Return, I show why the future ten head beast government will comprise ten heads of state, from ten regions of the earth that will initially be formed to include every nation on earth. It will be at this time that one of the ten heads or as I call them (heads of state) will be fatally wounded.

The opening of the first seal in Revelation 6:1-2, is the revealing of antichrist. When you realize that the antichrist will come from one of the ten global leadership positions, it makes sense that we will not truly know his identity until one of the ten leaders is fatally wounded and recovers as one coming back from the dead.

Revelation 13:3 (KJV) *"And I saw one of his heads as it were wounded to death; and the deadly wound was healed: and all the world wondered after the beast."* Now we see the arrival of Satan taking possession of a human host, one of the ten world leaders is now the Antichrist and will start to make war against the God's people.

As you read Revelation 13:5 it says how long this war will last, three and a half years. I see this supporting a mid-tribulation rapture. Revelation 13:5 (NIV) *"The beast was given a mouth to utter proud words and blasphemies and to exercise his authority for forty-two months."*

This next verse gives insight on the war on the saints and the scope of the Antichrist rule, which will include every nation. Revelation 13:7 (KJV) *"And it was given unto him to make war on the saints, and to overcome them: and power was given him over all kindred's, and tongues, and nations."*

Revelation 13:9-10 explains that during this three and a half year period it will not be an easy time for Christians. (KJV) *"If any man have an ear, let him hear. He that leadeth into captivity shall go into captivity: he that killeth with the sword must be killed with the sword. Here is the patience and the faith of the saints."*

The period we are entering is known as the seven year Great Tribulation. After the revealing of the Antichrist at the opening of the first seal, we see a second beast rising out of the earth, which many refer to as the false prophet. This person is the right hand man to the

Antichrist. Revelation 13:11-12 (KJV) *"And I beheld another beast coming up out of the earth; and he had two horns like a Lamb, and he spake as a dragon. And he exerciseth all the power of the first beast before him, and causeth the earth and them which dwell therein to worship the first beast, whose deadly wound was healed."*

One of the tasks of this second beast will be to enforce the system of the Antichrist. He will cause all to worship the Antichrist and take his mark. He will have all who refuse to comply put to death. It is obvious from God's Word that we must not take the mark of the beast.

Revelation 13:15b-17 (KJV) *"and cause that as many as would not worship the image of the beast should be killed. And he caused all, both small and great, rich and poor, free and bond, to receive a mark in their right hand, or in their foreheads: And that no man might buy or sell, save he that had the mark, or the name of the beast, or the number of his name."*

During a time when so much pressure is being brought to bear on the saints, God sends angels to preach the gospel to every nation. They will lead as many souls to Christ as possible, during these dark days.

Revelation 14:6-7 (KJV) *"And I saw another angel fly in the midst of heaven, having the everlasting gospel to preach unto them that dwell on the earth, and to every nation, and kindred, and tongue, and people, saying with a loud voice, Fear God, and give glory to him; for the hour of his judgment is come: and worship him that made heaven, and earth, and the sea, and the fountains of waters."*

Now the second seal is opened, a red horse whose rider was given power to take peace from the earth. Revelation 6:4 (KJV) *"Then another horse came out, a fiery red one. Its rider was given power to take peace from the earth and to make men slay each other. To him was given a large sword."*

When I read the description of both the second and the third seals, I imagine it is a time of great famine and anarchy. Lawlessness will abound and people will kill for a loaf of bread. It will be during this time that Christians who have seen this time coming and prepared, will be able to minister to some who are less fortunate and lead many to Christ.

Revelation 6:5-6 (KJV) "And w*hen the he had opened the third seal, I heard the third beast say, Come and see. And I beheld, and lo a black horse; and he that sat on him had a pair of balances in his hand. And I heard a voice in the midst of the four beasts say, A measure of wheat for a penny, and three measures of barley for a penny; and see thou hurt not the oil and the wine."*

Next the forth seal is opened and a pale horse is given power over a fourth of the earth. Because the word sword (a weapon of war) is used, I believe this will be war, contained to one fourth of the earth's area. Famine and plaques are the byproduct of war.

Revelation 6:7-8 (KJV) *"And when he opened the fourth seal, I heard the voice of the fourth beast say, Come and see. And I looked and behold a pale horse: and his name that sat on him was Death, and Hell followed with him. And power was given unto them over a fourth part of the earth, to kill with sword, and with hunger, and with death, and with the beasts of the earth."*

The fifth seal confirms this will be trying times for the saints. We must remember that no matter what happens to us, death has lost its sting for those in Christ Jesus, and God will bring us through anything that we have to endure. Revelation 6:9 (KJV) *"And when he had opened the fifth seal, I saw under the alter the souls of them that were slain for the word of God, and for the testimony which they held:"*

The sixth seal is the event that the saints have been waiting for. The sun goes dark and the moon does not give its normal light, and the stars fall from the sky. What is being described here is almost verbatim to what is described in Matthew 24:29-31 (KJV) *"Immediately after the tribulation of those days shall the sun be darkened, and the moon shall not give her light, and the stars shall fall from heaven, and the powers of the heavens shall be shaken: And then shall appear the sign of the Son of man in heaven: and then shall all the tribes of the earth mourn, and they shall see the Son of man coming in the clouds of heaven with power and great glory. And he shall send his angels with a great sound of a trumpet, and they shall gather together his elect from the four winds, from one end of heaven to the other."*

What I see at the opening of the sixth seal is what Joel in the Old Testament describes as the "Day of the Lord". He describes it as a great and terrible day. It is the day that the believers have been waiting for, when we would see the signs in the heavens signaling the coming of Jesus to gather His saints, thus making it a great day. For the unrepentant it will be a day when the ungodly will realize it is the time for the unleashing of God's wrath. Joel 2:30-31 (KJV) *"And I will show wonders in the heavens and in the earth, blood, and fire, and pillars of smoke.*

The sun shall be turned into darkness, and the moon into blood, before the great and the terrible day of the LORD come."

At this time when the saints are leaping for joy, knowing that the Rapture will happen soon, even though we still do not know the day or the hour of Christ's coming but the final sign has been given. It is now the time for the unrepentant to run and hide.

Revelation 6:15-17 (KJV) *"And the kings of the earth, and the great men, and the rich men, and the chief captains, and the mighty men, and every bondman, and every free man, hid themselves in the dens and in the rocks of the mountains; And said to the mountains and rocks, Fall on us, and hide us from the face of him that sitteth on the throne, and from the wrath of the Lamb: For the great day of his wrath is come; and who shall be able to stand?"*

As I continue this chronological commentary of Revelation, I need to point out that events described from the opening of the sixth seal in chapter six to the beginning of God's wrath in chapter eight, are overlapping the timeline to a degree. The Rapture is about to happen but the sealing of the 144,000 Jews happens before the rapture. We see the saints in white robes appearing in heaven in Revelation 7:9, this will be approximately the same timing as the silence we see at the throne in heaven as seen in Revelation 8:1.

As you read Revelation 7:1-3, an interesting event is happening. Four angels who are to bring great harm to the earth are told to hold off until the 144,000 Jews are sealed. These four angels could be the first four angels who are a part of the seven angels who deliver the seven trumpets of

God's wrath. If you will read the nature of the first four trumpets, each of these portions of God's wrath brings harm to the earth. This wrath is not to happen until the sealing of the 144,000 and the rapture of the elect. Revelation 7:1-2 (KJV) *"And after these things I saw four angels standing on the four corners of the earth, holding the four winds of the earth, that the wind should not blow on the earth , nor on the sea, nor on any tree. And I saw another angel ascending from the east, having the seal of the living God: and he cried with a loud voice to the four angels, to whom it was given to hurt the earth and the sea, Saying, Hurt not the earth, neither the sea, nor the trees, till we have sealed the servants of our God in their foreheads."*

It is also at this time that the two witnesses show up. We know that these two witnesses die before Christ's coming at the end of the Great Tribulation and we know that they are on the earth for three and a half years. This places their arrival just before the middle of the seven years of the Great Tribulation, making it possible that they will arrive a short time before the Rapture. The Bible indicates that during the time that the two witnesses are on the earth, they will have the power to stop the rain and call down plaques as often as they want to. They will be instruments of God to pinpoint God's wrath on the earth during the second half of the tribulation years. At this time God is also using His angels to pour out his wrath as well.

Revelation 11:3-6 (KJV) *"And I will give power unto my two witnesses, and they shall prophecy a thousand two hundred and three score days, clothed in sackcloth. These are the two olive trees, and the two candlesticks standing before the God of the earth. And if any man will hurt them, fire proceedeth out of their mouth, and devoureth their enemies: and if any man will hurt them, he must in this manner be killed. These have power to shut heaven that it rain not in the days of their prophecy: and have power over waters to turn them to blood, and to smite the earth with all plaques, as often as they will."*

The next portions of Scriptures that have been moved to their chronological location come from Revelation chapters 14 and 17. Both of these portions deal with the destruction of Mystery Babylon, with both showing the Rapture coming after this destruction. There is evidence in the Bible that the saints are on the earth at this time. The saints are admonished to patiently endure this time. This time will be a period when the saints will be subject to great trials during the war on the saints by the Antichrist, with many saints dying. This is confirmed in Daniel,7:21-22b (NIV) *"As I watched, this horn was waging war against the saints and defeating them, until the Ancient of Days came and pronounced judgment in favor of the saints of the Most High."* The Rapture will end the war on the saints. But don't lose heart, Daniel gives us an encouraging word as well in Daniel 11:32b (KJV) *"But the people that know their God shall be strong, and do exploits."*

Revelation 14: 12, 13 (KJV) *"Here is the patience of the saints: here are they that keep the commandments of God, and the faith of Jesus. And I heard a voice from heaven saying unto me, Write, Blessed are the dead which die in the Lord from henceforth: Yea, saith the Spirit, that they may rest from their labours; and their works do follow them."*

As you read the unfolding of the Scriptures I will be sharing, you will notice that the second angel is pronouncing that the Mystery Babylon is falling, and then the third angel is warning man not to worship the beast or to take his mark. This sequence shows that the saints are still on the earth after the fall of Mystery Babylon.

Revelation 14:8-10 (KJV) *"And there followed another angel, saying, Babylon is fallen, is fallen, that great city, because she made all nations drink of the wine of the wrath of her fornication. And the third angel followed them, saying with a loud voice, If any man worship the beast and his image, and receive his mark in his forehead, or in his hand, The same shall drink of the wine of the wrath of God, which is poured out without mixture into the cup of his indignation; and he shall be tormented with fire and brimstone in the presence of the holy angels, and in the presence of the Lamb;"*

Now we are going to look at the two and a half chapters from the second angelic interruption from Revelation 17:1 through 19:10. These chapters stay together as one chronological unit that is moved into its chronological location. Chapters 17 and 18 deal with Mystery Babylon that is referred to as a prostitute. The country being referred to here is guilty of corrupting other nations of the world and God is about to pour His judgment on this nation.

Revelation 17:1-2 (KJV) *"And there came one of the seven angels which had the seven vials, and talked to me, saying unto me, Come hither; I will show unto thee the judgment of the great whore that sitteth upon many waters: With whom the kings of the earth have committed fornication, and the inhabitants of the earth have been made drunk with the wine of her fornication."*

Not all will agree with my thoughts that the Great Whore or Mystery Babylon is the USA. I believe Revelation

17:15-16 describes the USA better than any other country and it says that the beast will be the one who will destroy this mystery country. As I mentioned in my book, The Window of the Lord's Return, the United States is the only super power nation that did not exist when the Bible was written, making it a mystery country.

Revelation 17:15-16 (KJV) *"And he saith unto me. The waters which thou sawest, where the whore sitteth, are peoples, and multitudes, and nations and tongues. And the ten horns which thou sawest upon the beast, these shall hate the whore, and shall make her desolate and naked, and shall eat her flesh, and burn her with fire."*

When you read Revelation chapter 18, it describes this mystery country with such detail that it sounds like America.

Revelation 18:15-18 (KJV) *"The merchants of these things, which were made rich by her, shall stand afar off for the fear of her torment, weeping and wailing, And saying, Alas. alas, that great city, that was clothed in fine linen, and purple, and scarlet, and decked with gold, and precious stones, and pearls! For in one hour so great riches is come to nought. And every ship master, and all the company in ships, and sailors, and as many as trade by sea, stood afar off, and cried when they saw the smoke of her burning, saying, What city is like unto this great city!*

The one exception I have to these verses pointing to America as Mystery Babylon is where it says that this nation would be guilty for the blood of prophets and the saints and many that are slain upon the earth. It makes me wonder and consider the possibility that in these last days America will turn against Christians in a great way.

Revelation 18:24 (KJV) *"And in her was found the blood of the prophets, and of saints, and of all that were slain upon the earth."*

Earlier in this study I explained why the second angelic interruption that includes Revelation 17:1-19:10 was one continuous piece of the puzzle and why it is moved as one unit. When you read the last portion of these Scripture verses from Revelation 19:1-10, you realize that from the destruction of Mystery Babylon to the end of this portion of Scripture, the Rapture has already taken place. Revelation 19:7-8 explains that the time for the marriage supper of the Lamb has come and this could not take place in heaven unless the bride is there as well.

Revelation 19:7-8 (KJV)*" Let us be glad and rejoice and give honour to him: for the marriage of the Lamb is come, and his wife hath made herself ready. And to her was granted that she should be arrayed in fine linen, clean and white: for the fine linen is the righteousness of saints."*

Earlier I covered Revelation 14:8-13, which also described the destruction of Mystery Babylon. Now I will continue where these verses left off and cover Revelation 14:14-16. These verses give further confirmation that the Rapture will happen following the destruction of Mystery Babylon.

Revelation 14:14-16 (KJV) *"And I looked and behold a white cloud, and upon the cloud one sat like unto the Son of man, having on his head a golden crown, and in his hand a sharp sickle. And another angel came out of the temple, crying with a loud voice to him that sat on the cloud, Thrust in thy sickle, and reap: for the time is come for thee to reap; for the harvest of the earth is ripe. And he that sat on the cloud thrust in his sickle on the earth; and the earth was reaped."*

The previous four portions of Revelation that I have been discussing have all been from the angelic interruptions that I have been repositioning in chronological order. The next portion I will be discussing will be going back to where we left off in Revelation chapter 7:9-8:1. These Scriptures start off talking about a great multitude that could not be numbered standing before the throne.

Revelation 7:9 (KJV) *"After this I beheld, and lo, a great multitude, which no man could number, of all nations, and kindreds, and people, and tongues, stood before the throne, and before the Lamb, clothed with white robes, and palms in their hands;"*

This verse has always given me the impression that these who are around the throne in white robes suddenly appeared there, convincing me that this is where we see the Rapture occur between the sixth and seventh seal. One reason why I have thought this is because one of the elders who is always at the throne has to ask the question, "Where did all these people in white robes come from?"

Revelation 7:13-*14* (KJV) *"And one of the elders answered, saying unto me, What are these which are arrayed in white robes? and whence came they? And I said unto him, Sir, thou knowest. And he said to me, These are they which came out of great tribulation, and have washed their robes, and made them white in the blood of the Lamb."* The elder is acknowledging that a number of saints that cannot be numbered have just arrived at the throne, having come out of the great tribulation. Realize that if the Rapture had already happened there would have been so many saints around the throne that these new ones could not have been noticed.

If you agree with me that this is the rapture of the saints, arriving at the throne of God, then you may also agree with me on my interpretation of Revelation 8:1(KJV) *"And when he opened the seventh seal, there was silence in heaven about the space of half an hour."* I see this as our arrival at the throne in heaven and we are standing before the throne in such awe that neither man, nor angelic beings can make a sound until our heavenly Father breaks the silence to welcome the bride of his Son to our new home.

This next portion of Scripture from Revelation 11:16-19 continues with the elders around the throne. When you read these verses it is easy to see how well they fit between Revelation 8:1 and Revelation 8:2. Revelation 8:1 is the time of silence in heaven where I see the arrival of the saints. Then we see the transition to the time of the wrath of God, where Revelation 8:2, shows the handing out of the trumpets for the beginning of God's wrath.

When you read Revelation 11:18-19, you will see it talks about this being the time for rewarding the children of God and the time for destroying those who have rejected Christ.

Revelation 11:18-19 (KJV) *"And the nations were angry, and thy wrath is come, and the time of the dead, that they should be judged, and that thou shouldest give reward unto thy servants the prophets, and to the saints, and them that fear thy name, small and great; and shouldest destroy them which destroy the earth. And the temple of God was opened in heaven, and there was seen in his temple the ark of his testament: and there were* **lightnings,** *and* **voices,** *and* **thunderings,** *and an* **earthquake,** *and great* **hail.** *"*

When you read the last verse above from chapter 11, where it describes events about to happen at the beginning of God's wrath, you will notice that these same events are covered in Revelation 8:5-7, describing what is about to happen leading up to the first trumpet judgment.

Revelation 8:5-7 (KJV) *"And the angel took the censer, and filled it with fire of the altar, and cast it into the earth: and there were **voices**, and **thunderings**, and **lightnings**, and an **earthquake**. And the seven angels which had the seven trumpets prepared themselves to sound. The first angel sounded, and there followed **hail** and fire mingled with blood, and they were cast upon the earth: and the third part of trees was burnt up, and all green grass was burnt up."*

As the seven trumpet judgments are taking place it is interesting that after the first four trumpet judgments an angel flies over the earth with a loud voice and proclaims a warning to those who inhabit the earth. This almost sounds like he is proclaiming the worst is yet to come. It gives me peace to know that while God's wrath is being poured out on the earth, the bride of Christ is resting in the safety of our new home.

Revelation 8:13 (KJV) *"And I beheld, and heard an angel flying through the midst of heaven, saying with a loud voice, Woe, woe, woe, to the inhabiters of the earth by reason of the other voices of the trumpet of the three angels, which are yet to sound!"*

As we study our way through the last three trumpets, we see the fifth trumpet is wicked. Scorpion creatures come out of the bottomless pit, which refers to hell and these creatures are commanded by a satanic being. Some, who teach that the saints will go through the wrath of God, teach that this period of wrath will be very short. When you read about just this trumpet of God's wrath, it says that these creatures will sting man with such a wicked sting that man will seek to die but will not be able to. Then it says that this portion of God's wrath will last for five months.

Revelation 9:1-6 (KJV) *"And the fifth angel sounded, and I saw a star fall from heaven unto the earth: and to him was given the key of the bottomless pit; and he opened the bottomless pit, and there arose a smoke out of the pit as the smoke of a great furnace; and the sun and the air were darkened by reason of the smoke of the pit. And there came out of the smoke locusts upon the earth: and unto them was given power, as the scorpions of the earth have power. And it was commanded them that they should not hurt the grass of the earth, neither any green thing, neither any tree; but only those men which have not the seal of God in their foreheads. And to them was given that they should not kill them, but that they should be tormented five months: and their torment was as the torment of a scorpion, when he striketh a man. And in those days shall men desire to die, and death shall flee from them."*

As we read the sixth trumpet, we see it involves four angels being released. As I read this it talks about these angels being prepared for an hour, and a day, and a month, and a year. This gives me the impression that this trumpet of God's wrath could last for a year. It goes on to talk of an army of 200 million and that during the period of this war that will come from this trumpet, a third part of mankind would die. This trumpet does not describe total destruction, like you would see from a nuclear war. This sixth seal is describing death by a strong military force, killing one third of mankind. It makes sence that this sixth trumpet would take a year to be accomplished.

Revelation 9:14-18 (KJV) *Saying to the sixth angel which had the trumpet, Loose the four angels which are bound in the great river Euphrates. And the four angels were loosed, which were prepared for an hour, and a day, and a month, and a year, for to slay the third part of men. And the number of the army of the horseman were two hundred thousand thousand: and I heard the number of them. And thus I saw the horses in the vision, and them that sat on them, having breastplates of fire, and of jacinth, and brimstone: and the heads of the horses were as the heads of lions; and out of their mouths issued fire and smoke, and brimstone. By these three was the third part of men killed, by the fire, and by the smoke, and by the brimstone, which issued out of their mouths."*

Revelation 10:7 speaks of the days of the seventh trumpet, but it does not identify what this judgment entails. It almost sounds like the seventh trumpet signals events happening in heaven concerning God's elect. If you will review the seventh seal, it was a mystery that I believe also involved events in heaven concerning the saints.

Revelation 10:7 (KJV) *"But in the days of the voice of the seventh angel, when he shall begin to sound, the mystery of God should be finished, as he hath declared to his servants the prophets."*

Then as we read Revelation 11:15, this verse also sounds like this seventh trumpet signals an event that is happening in heaven, possibly tied to the marriage supper of the Lamb.

Revelation 11:15 (KJV) *"And the seventh angel*

sounded; and there were great voices in heaven, saying, The kingdoms of this world are become the kingdoms of our Lord, and of his Christ; and he shall reign for ever and ever."

We are now at the place in time when the seven last plaques will be released. There are some who say these seven bowls of God's wrath are all that is the wrath of God, saying that the trumpets are not the wrath of God. If you will read in Revelation 15:1, it says the seven angels have the seven last plaques. If these are the last plaques, then there had to be other plaques before them.

Another interesting point is in Revelation 15:2, it talks of the redeemed and the overcomers having a great worship service in heaven while the seven angels are about to be sent to the earth with the last seven plaques.

Revelation 15:1-3 (KJV) *"And I saw another sign in heaven, great and marvelous, seven angels having the seven last plaques; for in them is filled up the wrath of God. And I saw as it were a sea of glass mingled with fire: and them that had gotten the victory over the beast, and over his image, and over his mark, and over the number of his name, stand on the sea of glass, having the harps of God. And they sing the song of Moses the servant of God, and the song of the Lamb, saying, Great and marvelous are thy works, Lord God Almighty; just and true are thy ways, thou King of saints."*

After the completion of the seven bowls of God's wrath, it is now the time that Jesus will return to win the victory from Satan that was ordained to be. Jesus returns on a white horse with the armies of heaven following close behind. The saints in white robes are riding white horses so we can witness the greatness of Jesus Christ putting down evil and setting up His reign on the earth.

Revelation 19:11-16 *"And I saw heaven opened, and behold a white horse; and he that sat upon him was called Faithful and True, and in righteousness he doth judge and make war. His eyes were as a flame of fire, and on his head were many crowns; and he had a name written, that no man knew, but he himself. And he was clothed with a vesture dipped in blood: and his name is called The Word of God. And the armies which were in heaven followed him upon white horses, clothed in fine linen, white and clean. And out of his mouth goeth a sharp sword, that with it he should smite the nations: and he shall rule them with a rod of iron: and he treadeth the winepress of the fierceness and wrath of Almighty God. And he hath on his vesture and on his thigh a name written, KING OF KINGS and LORD OF LORDS."*

Now as we continue this chronological commentary of the book of Revelation, we go back to Revelation 14:17-20, and we see the angels, the warriors of God's army go into action to harvest the unrepentant and wipe out the armies assembled for the battle of Armageddon.

Revelation 14:17-20 (KJV) *"And another angel came out of the temple which is in heaven, he also having a sharp sickle. And another angel came out from the altar, which had power over fire; and cried with a loud cry to him that had the sharp sickle, saying, Thrust in thy sharp sickle, and gather the clusters of the vine of the earth; for her grapes are fully ripe. And the angel thrust in his sickle into the earth, and gathered the vine of the earth, and cast it into the great winepress of the wrath of God. And the winepress was trodden without the city, and blood came out of the winepress, even unto the horse bridles, by the space of a thousand and six hundred furlongs."*

As we continue reading Revelation chapter19, we see all the players coming together for the final battle. Revelation 19:19-21 (KJV) *"And I saw the beast, and the kings of the earth, and their armies, gathered together to make war against him that sat on the horse, and against his army. And the beast was taken, and with him the false prophet that wrought miracles before him, with which he deceived them that had received the mark of the beast, and them that worshipped his image. These both were cast alive into a lake of fire burning with brimstone. And the remnant were slain with the sword of him that sat upon the horse, which sword proceeded out of his mouth: and all the fouls were filled with their flesh."*

As I read Revelation14:1-5, I see the final pieces coming together. Jesus is meeting with the 144,000 Jews that were sealed for a special purpose. This meeting is taking place on Mount Zion. This could not have happened until Christ's return. Now the battle of Armageddon is over, as Jesus meets with the 144,000 it appears they are translated to the throne of God to join in a special worship service before the throne.

Revelations 14: 1-3 (KJV) *"And I looked, and, lo, a Lamb stood on the mount Zion, and with him an hundred forty and four thousand, having his Father's name written in their foreheads. And I heard a voice from heaven, as the voice of many waters, and as the voice of a great thunder: and I heard the voice of harpers harping with their harps: And they sung as it were a new song before the throne, and before the four beasts, and the elders: and no man could learn that song but the hundred and forty four thousand, which were redeemed from the earth."*

As we read the rest of the Book of Revelation, the final events are falling together. Revelation 20:4 is a time of judgment and I believe a time of rewards for those who went through the trials of the tribulation period. Those who did not wavier; even in death. We are now about to enter the one thousand years of peace.

Revelation 20:4, *"And I saw thrones and they sat upon them: and judgment was given unto them; and I saw the souls of them that were beheaded for the witness of Jesus, and for the word of God, and which had not worshipped the beast, neither his image, neither had received his mark upon their foreheads, or in their hands; and they lived and reigned with Christ a thousand years."*

It is hard to imagine that man could ever be deceived again but after the one thousand years of peace, the Bible says that Satan will be released one last time to deceive the nations. You have to realize that during the one thousand years of peace that the earth will be repopulated with mortals and it's like they will have an opportunity to either stand with God or to stand with the devil for one last uprising against God.

Revelation 20:7-10 (KJV) *"And when the thousand years are expired, Satan shall be loosed out of his prison, And shall go out to deceive the nations which are in the four quarters of the earth, Gog and Magog, to gather them together to battle: the number of whom is as the sand of the sea. And they went up on the breath of the earth, and compassed the camp of the saints about, and the beloved city: and fire came down from God out of heaven, and devoured them. And the devil that deceived them was cast into the lake of fire and brimstone, where the beast and the false prophet are and shall be tormented day and night for ever and ever."*

Once the 1000 years of peace are over, and Satan is cast into the lake of fire for eternity, at this time all who have ever died will be judged according to their works. Without the forgiveness of God through the blood of his Son Jesus Christ, our name would never make it into the Lambs Book of Life, and we would be found wanting and condemned for ever.

Revelations 20: 11-15 (KJV) *" And I saw a great white throne, and him that sat on it, from whose face the earth and heaven fled away; and there was found no place for them. And I saw the dead, small and great, stand before God; and the books were opened: and another book was opened, which is the book of life: and the dead were judged out of those things which were written in the books, according to their works. And the sea gave up the dead which were in it; and death and hell delivered up the dead which were in them: and they were judged every man according to their works. And death and hell were cast into the lake of fire. This is the second death. And whosoever was not found written in the book of life was cast into the lake of fire."*

After the final judgment of man is over, God's Word says that God will create a new heavens and a new earth. The Bible actually says that the old heavens will roll up like a scroll. The splendor of what God will create for us as our new eternal home will be beyond our imagination. These promises are a sure thing. After all that our God has promised those who will remain faithful to the end, we need to examine our hearts and determine that we will follow God's will for our life to the end.

Revelation 21:1-5 (KJV) *"And I saw a new heaven and a new earth: for the first heaven and the first earth were passed away; and there was no more sea. And I John saw the holy city, New Jerusalem, coming down from God out of heaven, prepared as a bride adorned for her husband. And I heard a great voice out of heaven saying, Behold, the tabernacle of God is with men, and he will dwell with them, and they shall be his people, and God himself shall be with them and be their God. And God shall wipe away all tears from their eyes; and there shall be no more death, neither sorrow, nor crying, neither shall there be any more pain: for the former things are passed away. And he that sat on the throne said, Behold, I make all things new. And he said unto me, Write: for these words are true and faithful."*

I am concluding my commentary at this point, but I would encourage you to study on. The last two chapters go on to describe the new earth and the New Jerusalem that will come down from the heavens. Then the book of Revelation continues to describe what it will be like in our new home.

Eternal life will be so awesome, well worth any suffering for Christ that we will go through in this life.

Reading guide for any Translation

To read the book of Revelation in any preferred translation, you can use the list of Scripture references below to bring you through the Book of Revelation in chronological order, in the translation of your choice.

1. Revelation 1:1......5:14

2. Revelation 12:1....13:2

3. Revelation 6:1.......6:2

4. Revelation 13:3...13:18

5. Revelation 14:6.....14:7

6. Revelation 6:3........7:8

7. Revelation 11:1...11:14

8. Revelation 14:8....14:13

9. Revelation 17:1...19:1-10

10. Revelation 14:14 ...14:16

11. Revelation 7:9 ....8:1

12. Revelation 11:16.... 11:19

13. Revelation 8:2........10:11

14. Revelation 11:15

15. Revelation 15:1....16:21

16. Revelation 19:11... 19:16

17. Revelation 14:17...14:20

18. Revelation 19:17....20:3

19. Revelation 14:1.....14:5

20. Revelation 20:4...22:21

Closing Commentary

After reading and studying the Book of Revelation in chronological order, the case for a Mid-Tribulation rapture as illuminated in Revelation chapters 7 and 8, is so strong that the other teachings on the timing of the rapture have been greatly diminished. I believe that if the Book of Revelation would have been written in chronological order in the beginning, the other teachings on the timing of the rapture would never have made sense in light of the chronological reading of the Book of Revelation.

In my first book, The Window of the Lord's Return, I make a strong case for a Mid-tribulation rapture. I believe this second study sheds further light on the timing of the Rapture. In fact if I may be so bold, I believe this study validates the Mid-tribulation rapture. This being the case, I would like to bring up a discussion on the need to prepare for the last days.

If you believe as I do that not only America, but all nations are heading for an appointment with the end times and a coming global one world government. It seems hard to imagine America giving up its independence and being a part of this end time's prophecy from the book of Revelation, but the Bible does say that the Antichrist will rule over every nation and America is a nation.

With the American and global economies standing on shaky ground, it is not hard for me to believe that an event could happen that could trigger a panic on Wall Street and a panic on Main Street. This may lead to either a slow slide or a rapid slide into something worse than the Great Depression of the 1930's. With the irresponsible spending of our leaders, you don't have to be a rocket scientist to see the day could soon come when we witness the collapse of our dollar.

If you see this global collapse as a soon coming event, I believe that as a Christian, we will have a divine purpose for going through part of the Great Tribulation; it should compel us to take some important steps to be prepared for these coming days. I have said this before and it deserves repeating. It took Noah many years to prepare. He was warned that great storm clouds would come and unless he built an ark, he and his family would be in trouble. The Bible says that Noah built an ark in holy fear for the saving of his family.

The main point I want to make is, Noah was building an ark while the sun was shining, and he was laughed at and was probably told that he was a few bricks short of a full load. When the rain started to fall and the water was rising, Noah was a hero to his family. If you want to be a hero to your family, then don't wait to build your ark of safety. Some are saying the economy will recover and we will see great prosperity again. I praise God that He is allowing us more time to get ready. We have been seeing the signs of Christ's coming, going back to the rebirth of Israel in 1948. Jesus warned that people can discern the signs in the sky and know the weather for the following day, but most can't recognize the signs God gave us for His return.

God has told us to watch and be ready. If we wait to take steps to prepare for the last days, it will be too late. When it becomes evident to all that the dollar will collapse, at that point everyone will take steps to prepare and as they say, you will be a day late and a dollar short.

Having ample food and water will be important, but the most important preparation concerns your soul. If you have not accepted Jesus as your Lord and Savior, these easy steps will put you in right standing with God. Have you truly asked God to forgive your sins and asked Jesus into your heart?

1. Admit you are a sinner and repent.

(Romans 3:10 NIV), "As it is written: There is no one righteous, not even one."

(Romans 3:23 NIV), "For all have sinned and fall short of the glory of God."

(Luke 5:32 NIV), "I have not come to call the righteous, but sinners to repentance

2. Believe in the Lord Jesus Christ.

(John 3:16 NIV), "For God so loved the world that He gave his one and only Son, that whosoever believes in him shall not perish but have eternal life."

3. Confess or declare that Jesus is the Lord of your life.

(Romans 10:9 NIV), "That if you confess with your mouth, 'Jesus is Lord,' and believe in your heart that God raised him from the dead, you shall be saved."

The Sinner's Prayer

If you would like God to forgive all your sins and make Jesus Christ the Lord of your life, then stop here and say this prayer to God. (Prayer is simply talking to God.)

Dear Heavenly Father, I know I am a sinner. I believe Jesus Christ died on the cross for me. Please forgive me of all my sins. Jesus, please come into my heart and wash my sins away. Please be the Lord of my life and help me to live for you every day. I ask this in Jesus name. Amen.

The Bible says when a sinner repents and makes Jesus his Lord, the angels in heaven rejoice.

A word of warning is advised at this point. As we read in the story of the ten virgins, not all who call themselves Christians will make it to heaven. Knowing about Jesus and the plan of salvation is no guarantee of making it to heaven. When we arrive in heaven, the greatest surprise will be seeing people we did not think would make it. And just as surprising will be the absence of those we thought would be there. The Bible says Jesus knocks on the door of our hearts and wants to come in and live with us. The important thing to realize is God wants our hearts, not just our minds. Head knowledge about salvation does not save us, but sincerely allowing God to forgive and wash our sins away will allow God to give you a new heart. When your heart is changed, people will notice you have been changed and made into a new person in Christ. This is called being "Born Again."

I get letters from time to time asking for advice on how to prepare. I try to give good advice but sometimes it is not easy to give that good of an answer. One of those questions came from an elderly lady who asked me,

"How do I prepare when I don't have much money?" As I have pondered of how to answer this question, I have come up with some thoughts I would like to share, for all of us to consider.

Because most Christians today believe we will see an early rapture before things get real bad, most of these who believe this are not taking steps to prepare. When events happen that will bring us over the fiscal cliff, causing panic to spread around the globe, it will be too late to prepare. I believe coming events will shake the faith of many to the core. Good Christian people will not be able to prepare for a long period of the coming Great Tribulation. Churches will not be able to prepare to feed those who do not have the resources to take care of themselves. This reality has triggered a number of thoughts I will conclude with.

One of the thoughts I had concerning the elderly lady who asked me the question, "How do I prepare, when I do not have financial resources?" The story in the Old Testament came to mind. There was this widow and her son who was down to their last meal and the prophet Elijah shows up hungry and asked her to feed him.

Read her response and the outcome, 1 Kings 17:12-16 (NIV) *"As surely as the Lord your God lives; she replied, "I don't have any bread-only a handful of flour in a jar and a little oil in a jug. I am gathering a few sticks to take home and make a meal for myself and my son that we may eat it- and die." Elijah said to her, "Don't be afraid. Go home and do as you have said. But first make a small cake of bread for me from what you have and bring it to me, and then make something for yourself and your son. For this is what the Lord, the God of Israel, says: "The jar of flour will not be used up and the jug of oil will not run dry until the day the Lord sends rain on the land." She went away and did as Elijah had told her. So there was food every day for Elijah and for the woman and her family. For the jar of flour was not used up and the jug of oil did not run dry, in keeping with the word of the Lord spoken by Elijah."*

Please don't think this is a brush off answer that I would say, "If you have great faith, you will have food." No, there is a principle here I would like to point out. During the coming famines of the last days there will be multitudes that will not be able to buy food because we have refused the mark of the beast and the system of the Antichrist. Many Christians will get down to their last meal. We can hide and eat the last of our food alone and then die as this widow was preparing to do or we can invite some hungry neighbor over and share our last meal and share the gospel. The Bible says in the last days we will do exploits for God. The greatest exploit we can do is leading a lost soul to Jesus and bring them into eternity with us.

After putting these thoughts down, another thought came to me, "What can churches do to prepare and help feed the hungry during this time?" If a church thinks they can store enough food for every member of their church along with everyone in the community that hears that the church has food, this could be a daunting task. I do believe many miracles of provision will happen in the last days. Remember Jesus fed the 5000 with only a few loaves of bread and a few fish, and there was food left over for another meal. In all of the miracles of provision that I am aware of, God multiplied something that they already had. As a church, I believe you must do something. One viable plan would be for the churches to store food for the coming economic collapse, with a great outreach in mind. If a church would take some steps to prepare, then when this event hits, they would be prepared for the biggest church potluck in the history of their church. At this time people will be hungry, scared and looking for answers. When this great banquet is prepared you will open your doors to all in your community to receive a meal and a message on the coming of the Lord Jesus.

My last closing thoughts have to do with a movie I recently watched called, "Hunger Games." This movie was very futuristic, Orwellian and full of the spirit of antichrist. In this future time movie, two people from the age of twelve to eighteen where chosen from twelve districts each year. They would be transported to a controlled wilderness area and released to survive to the last man standing. The winner would be given special rewards, including rewards for the district they came from. To win you would need to use survival skills and be able to fight off the others who would want you to die so they could live.

As I was watching this movie, it dawned on me that Christians could take on this same attitude. That the winner is the one who survives until the Rapture takes us home. Those Christians who take this attitude, an attitude that says I will survive no matter what I have to do, will have missed the point. When Paul and Silas were in prison they counted it joy to suffer for Christ, the one who gave his life that they could live for eternity. It was this attitude of Paul and Silas that led to the jailer getting saved and his whole family as well.

Doesn't the Bible say in Matthew 20:16, "he that is last shall be first and he that is first shall be last."? What

I see in this verse is, those who put themselves first will be last, but those who put the needs of others first will receive the greatest reward. It is all about being a servant to the needs of others.

Please don't think I am super spiritual. I struggle with the very things I am writing about. I want to prepare for my family but I know I must not be self-centered. I must consider the needs of others for whom Christ died. It is my prayer that when the time of tribulation comes rushing in on us, my attitude and actions will be pleasing to God. It is my prayer that I will hear the words of Jesus. Matthew 25:23, *"Well done, good and faithful servant."*

Please do not judge me for the conclusions of which I have arrived. Study the Word of God for yourselves and ask the Holy Spirit to reveal the truth of His Word to you. I believe we should follow the example set by the Bereans. Acts 17:11, (NIV) *"Now the Bereans were of more noble character than the Thessalonians, for they received the message with great eagerness and examined the Scriptures every day to see if what Paul said was true."*

God Bless you as you search God's Word for truth,

John Shorey

Reorder information on the following page

To order additional copies of this book
Order online at:

www.tribulationtruth.com

01-03 copies $12.99 each, plus $4.00 S/H

4-10 copies $9.99 each, plus $8.00 S/H

11-20 copies 8.99 each, plus $12.95 S/H

21-30 copies $7.99 each, plus $15.95 S/H

Thank you for your support to this ministry

Speaking availability

John Shorey is available to speak, preach or teach the insights God has directed him to write. For more information or to schedule a speaking engagement, He may be contacted through the following website:

www.tribulationtruth.com